I love this book. It fills me with joy in its beauty and subtle dharma. God is there with a child eating macaroni or in the flight over Niagara Falls. The poems are so clear, lovely and evocative.

—Rabbi Rachel Cowan
author of *Wise Aging: Living with Joy, Resilience and Spirit*

This book is like taking a contemplative stroll with a wise teacher who occasionally shares a story, a poem, a laugh, a prayer and a psalm along the way. Each page whispers to us "wake up" and embrace the stranger within us and around us.

—Rev. Dr. Lawrence Peers
Unitarian Universalist minister

"Ordinary" moments—unintentionally saying something unkind or calming a hungry child—become extraordinary when Rabbi Weinberg tunes her heart to meditation and her pen to gentle eloquence. An excellent companion for our own ordinary/extraordinary moments.

—Rabbi Arthur Waskow
author of *Godwrestling—Round 2*

With honesty, humor, and gentleness, Sheila Weinberg invites us to join in examining our lives. Drawing on Jewish and Buddhist teachings, life stories, and conversations with her grandchildren, she offers a very timely guide to enriching the spiritual, political, and personal dimensions of our experience.

—Martha Ackelsberg
William R. Kenan, Jr. Professor emerita of Government
Smith College

A prescient and persuasively timely collection, *God Loves the Stranger* inspires and challenges us to deepen our spiritual sensibility as we act for radical justice in our country and our world. Weinberg embodies and expresses a profoundly honest, clear, personal and moving call to wholeness, love and justice.

—Rabbi Nancy Flam
Senior Program Director, Institute for Jewish Spirituality

Most of us long for a friend who knows us well and loves us anyway, a companion who can listen deeply and offer insightful responses, and can double up with laughter over the delicious absurdities of her, and our humanness. Sheila Weinberg is that friend; *God Loves the Stranger* reveals why she is a beloved mindfulness teacher and trusted Spiritual Director. This rich and courageous collection invites us to both imagine and inhabit a world where we are no longer strangers to ourselves or to one another.

Rabbi Sue Levi Elwell, PhD
Editor, *The Open Door Haggadah* and *Chapters of the Heart: Jewish Women Sharing the Torah of Our Lives*

GOD
LOVES
THE
STRANGER

STORIES,
POEMS,
PRAYERS

SHEILA
PELTZ
WEINBERG

WHITE RIVER PRESS   AMHERST, MASSACHUSETTS

God Loves the Stranger: Stories, Poems, Prayers

First published March 2017

White River Press
PO Box 3561
Amherst, MA 01004
whiteriverpress.com

Book and cover design: Rebecca S. Neimark, Twenty-Six Letters
Cover photographs © 2017 Kristen Joyce, iStock.com/elwynn1130, iStock.com/ malyugin, iStock.com/Neustockimages, iStock.com/PeopleImages, iStock.com/ VSanandhakrishna, iStock.com/ZoneCreative

© 2007 John Makransky, *Awakening Through Love*. Reprinted by arrangement with Wisdom Publications, Inc., wisdompubs.org

ISBN: 978-1-887043-31-1 (print)
      978-1-887043-32-8 (ebook)

Library of Congress Cataloging-in-Publication Data
Names: Weinberg, Sheila Peltz, author.
Title: God loves the stranger / Sheila Peltz Weinberg.
Description: Amherst, Massachusetts : White River Press, 2017.
Identifiers: LCCN 2016044855 (print) | LCCN 2016045457 (ebook) | ISBN
    9781887043311 (pbk. : alk. paper) | ISBN 9781887043328 ()
Subjects: LCSH: Self-actualization (Psychology)—Religious aspects—Judaism. |
    Self-realization—Religious aspects—Judaism.
Classification: LCC BM729.S44 W45 2017 (print) | LCC BM729.S44 (ebook) |
DDC
    296.7—dc23
LC record available at https://lccn.loc.gov/2016044855

to Sylvia Boorstein, my beloved friend and teacher

The nature of all persons, like your own nature, is cognizance and openness, endowed with innate capacities of goodness and wisdom, but patterned . . . into self-clinging chains of thought and reaction. All persons, like yourself, need and fundamentally deserve enduring reverence, love, and care as they undergo the struggles, joys, and desperations of living and dying together in this world. No one is merely what our narrow, self-centered thoughts make of him or her— merely a "stranger," merely "unlikeable," merely "my friend," merely contemptible, merely impressive or unimpressive, merely stupid or smart. Everyone is *much* more than that. And when we hear this teaching . . . deep down we know it. We recognize this truth.

—John Makransky,
Awakening Through Love, pp. 106–7

TABLE OF CONTENTS

INTRODUCTION

God Loves the Stranger
—Deuteronomy 10:18

When I take these words deeply into my being, my flesh and blood, there is enormous relief. I am no longer struggling to protect the limited ideas I have about who I am. I am no longer projecting endlessly limited ideas of who you are. I am free. No one is a stranger. Everyone including my so-called enemies is an infinitely complex and precious creature. My labels, categories, and strategies to protect myself from them are paltry in comparison with their sacred mystery.

In our everyday lives, the stranger is sometimes the refugee, sometimes the person of color, age, youth, accent, small or large body, deafness, blindness, baldness, or different view, different neighborhood, different family or lover, profession, or power. There is no limit to who the stranger can be. In fact, some of our most challenging strangers may be those we live with and those we have loved or tried to love.

To see and understand this is the purpose of practice. To provide the social and cultural conditions to deepen this understanding is the purpose of all efforts toward justice and peace. The idea that God loves the stranger unites our inner work and our outer work. The inner work shines light, again and again, on the false conclusions I draw about my self. When I look carefully, calmly, through the lens of divine love, I see that I am none of these labels. I am indeed a stranger even to my own awareness. Now I inhabit this mood, this moment of joy or sadness, fear or envy, generosity, clarity, or confusion. Then it changes.

When I remember that God loves the stranger, the very category of stranger ceases to have meaning. God's love is undifferentiated, unconfined, unlimited. It is an expression of the reality of deepest unity and interconnection of all life in the cosmos, drawn from a single source, ever spiraling, expanding, and returning. All other beings are working with their own limited ideas of who they are and who I am, just as I am working with mine. There is no difference that is substantial.

When I am receptive to the love of the stranger who lives within my own heart and mind, I can extend this love to the other, to one I think I know and to one I do not know. Without exception. This attitude aspires to create a world that is moving toward a more equitable distribution of resources and opportunities, a world of respect and sharing, a world saturated with the recognition of unity and love. This is a world where Black lives really matter and a refugee is received with interest, care, and empathy.

These stories and poems, teachings and meditative exercises are a product of a spiritual practice both in formal settings and in the ordinary life of a seeker, a Jewish woman in her eighth decade of life, a wife, a mother, and a grandmother who is trying to let God love her. It is my hope that they inspire you toward your own practices and your own embrace of the stranger that God loves.

PART I

SUFFERING,
DESIRE,
AVERSION,
AND DELUSION

At any moment in my life I might experience discomfort. It could be physical—too hot, too cold, too noisy; or it might be emotional—I get frightened, annoyed, confused, agitated, angry, saddened. It might be mental—thoughts and stories arise in the mind that bode ill for the future or remind me of wretched things that happened in the past. Not infrequently, imaginative narratives unfold in my mind about my unworthiness or inadequacy.

This is life. It happens. Growing in wisdom and compassion is about tracking these manifestations without disliking them. We learn over time to accept that this is how we are wired. Running away is futile. Getting into conflict with reality is a lost cause.

These feelings and thoughts are the strangers that manifest all the time in a regular life. Our practice is to learn how to treat these strangers with love. "Do not oppress the stranger," we are told in the Torah. We discover that the stranger needs our love. The stranger needs God's love.

TARGET: A MOMENT OF CHESED

Sometimes spiritual teaching emerges in the moment. It is an act of grace. There are many opportunities in our ordinary interactions, especially with children, to open to a perspective that heals and frees rather than deepens tension, hurt, or conflict. The core mandate of a Jewish spirituality is teaching our children: *"V'shinantam l'vanecha"* (Deuteronomy 6:7 and the daily prayer book). This is a teaching centered in love and spirituality rather than in mastery of content. It teaches trust in the knowledge that one is safe in this moment because this, too, is a holy moment. It teaches that the source of life's contentment is being in connection to the whole, the unity of life itself, in being *with* Being, rather than in having more, doing more, or even knowing more.

Having grandchildren has opened me to wonderful spiritual teaching and learning opportunities. I loved being a parent but this is completely different. The grandchildren break my heart open. Although they seem so innocent and so vulnerable, grandchildren have all kinds of wondrous ways to have power over adults who in size, authority, and resources appear so much more powerful. This is an interesting nexus for spiritual teaching.

My husband and I were taking care of our then five-year-old granddaughter who was free after a half day of kindergarten. She really wanted to go to lunch at Ikea where they have videos, a game room for kids, and yummy fish sticks, French fries, and chocolate milk. So we took her. We also wanted to buy a gift for her brother, who was turning two. We could not find anything for him at Ikea, so after lunch and some playtime we went to

Target. We found an ideal basketball set very quickly, and our granddaughter asked me if I could get her something. I knew she needed a dark turtleneck for her school uniform, so we found one in her size. Then she said she needed new pj's. "Fine," I said, and we picked up a fuzzy one-piece in a princess print. Then she asked for other things—a toy, an umbrella, a doll, a set of this or that. I did not want to get her anything else, and as she kept asking, I noticed that I was becoming less patient. She said, "C'mon Grandma, just one thing and then I will stop asking." I was annoyed with her; I didn't want to give in. But I didn't want her to be upset either. Yikes.

That was when the moment of *chesed* descended. I paused. I took a few deep breaths. I bent down so we were eye to eye. This is very important. I said, "Honey, I know how it feels when you come to a place like this. Everything is calling to you. Everything looks so shiny and beautiful and makes you feel like you really want it. I know this feeling too. The people who own this store are counting on you feeling this way." She nodded. She knew what I was talking about. I said, "Let's just feel what this feels like." I paused. "It is desire, wanting, needing to have something. I feel it too. But, you and I both know that, as soon as we buy whatever it is and we think it will make us feel great and happy, almost right away, we want something else. Then, as soon as we get it home, or pretty soon, it ends up in some corner or in a pile somewhere." She became quiet. She looked at me with her enormous dark brown eyes, and she kept quiet. I paid for the toy, the pj's, and the shirt. We walked out of Target. Just as we got to the door, she said, "If it were my birthday, you would have gotten me something, right, Grandma?" "Yes, sweetheart."

In *Pirkei Avot* 4:28 Rabbi Elazar Ha-Kappar taught, "Envy, lust, and honor will ruin a person's life." How do we cultivate skills to meet the envy, lust, and craving for honor that beset us our whole lives? How do we remember that there is a power in the world that is stronger than these forces? Our culture is filled with invitations to increase desire for the ephemeral and the insubstantial, and for constant external validations of our worth. From an early age we are schooled in relentless comparing and competition. Spiritual training is countercultural. I had asked my five-year-old granddaughter to take a step outside the competitive consumer culture, to know that she was okay in this moment, to recognize the delusion that she would be satisfied by having the next thing.

REDIRECT THE WANTING MIND

From wanting pleasure to wanting peace,
from wanting pain to cease
to wanting warm, loving awareness of all things,
from getting it right
to pure intention,
from rushing
to concepts, judgments, and conclusions
to a mind filled with wonder and curiosity.

RELEASING THE STRIVING

I was once a passenger in a car accident. No one else was hurt, but I had a very wounded chest for some weeks. After about a month of pain—bargaining with my own mind whether to be tough or soft; taking drugs, not taking drugs; hanging out most of the time with a hot water bottle—I went to California to teach at an Institute for Jewish Spirituality (IJS) Hevraya (Alumni) retreat. I knew I couldn't teach yoga, and I asked my friends to keep an eye on me and on my penchant to overdo.

On the second morning of this retreat, there is always a silent walk through the hills to see the sunrise and have an ecstatic *davenning* with two great prayer leaders. I knew I shouldn't go: I needed the sleep; it would be cold on top of the mountain; I barely had the energy to teach my own class. But I felt guilty. I felt that not going would be a slight to the leaders. And I was afraid to miss the group experience. It was obvious to me that I was stranded between my wholesome and unwholesome desires, and it was quite painful and constricting. I needed help and no one was there. I couldn't just do the letting go. I needed a source of compassion to surround me and guide me. I opened in prayer asking my higher power to remove the guilt, the desire, the obsessive need to be everywhere and to allow me to rest in this moment of healing and care. Amazingly, I experienced being heard. It wasn't a voice from on high; rather, I knew ease of mind and heart. It was a moment of mindfulness, which is a moment of compassion. This allowed for the release of attachment to the ego and to the unwholesome, striving story of myself. When I got out of the center of the story, calm and peace arose. And, by the way, no one mentioned that they felt bad because I wasn't there.

KOAN

Nothing to get or get rid of.
Nothing to have.
Nothing to know.
Nothing to do.
Nothing to be.
Nothing to prove.
Resting in space.
Here.
Now,
Wow.
Let the retreat do me. Whatever it wants.
Wherever it goes.
Let it dissolve me.

KARAOKE ON THE SABBATH

Right Action is a true Sabbath practice if we think of it as withdrawing from the marketplace and finding ease and peace with what we have instead of what we think we need. It is particularly hard for people to desist from errands on Shabbat and from the electronic universe we inhabit that continuously revs up our desire for something better, newer, more. Right Action is the cultivation of Shabbat consciousness—desiring the well being of others; honesty, contentment, generosity, and fidelity. Our time on retreat, even if it is not Shabbat, is also a Shabbat practice.

Renunciation leads us to explore what is truly wholesome, satisfying, and joyful. Renunciation gives us a glimpse into impermanence, which is liberating. If we don't indulge desire, it does pass, as long as we don't judge it harshly and, instead, open in kindness to this very desire. Sometimes the path to liberation leads through developing the capacity to stay with discomfort. In her book, *On the Run*, sociologist Alice Goffman tells the story of having spent six years living with poor inner-city African Americans in Philadelphia. Many in this community spend their lives hopelessly entangled in a life of poverty and violence, perennially pursued and persecuted by the criminal justice system. Alice is a white, privileged, highly educated young woman, half Jewish, who manages to delve deeply into the quality and structure of this community that is very different from hers. In a lengthy discussion of her research methodology she writes: ". . . my task was not to let my comfort level guide the inquiry." The brilliance of this book is a direct product of her methodology and as she says:

". . . I tried to be careful not to give greater weight to the places and situations where I was most at ease." Wow. That is impressive.

I had a recent experience with a similar teaching. When my beloved sister-in-law turned seventy-five, her four children and ten grandchildren (the oldest was nine years old) decided to give her a surprise pizza party at a Karaoke club. It was important for us to attend, though the round trip from Philadelphia to New Haven was going to make for a long day. It was on the eighth day of Pesach, and on a Shabbat, but as a Reconstructionist, I was okay with traveling. So we went. Although it was a pizza party, one of the cousins thoughtfully brought a box of matzahs. But the four-hour party featured high-volume music. Very high-volume. At one point, I found myself irritated, constricted, and wondering how I was going to last. I took a break and walked around the block. I came back and felt my mind getting tighter. I tried to "hold it together" but finally, I spilled my discomfort to my husband, Maynard (who, of course, already knew from my body language that I was in exile), and he said, "Look, this party makes my sister very happy. That's what it is for. If you don't like it, that's okay. It's not your party." I was struck by the wisdom of his comment and the call for my relaxation, Right Action, non-conflict, loving kindness toward myself, who was the one in pain in this case. I remembered when our five-year-old granddaughter Hadassah had to find peace at not receiving a birthday present on her brother's birthday. How alike we were in this moment of desire and dissatisfaction. It was also a reminder of impermanence, generosity, and letting go of the idea that feeling comfortable is the only gateway to generosity. Releasing my bad attitude was really the holiest thing I could do. Shabbos is the reminder of holiness, wholeness in creation, so perhaps this was a true moment of Shabbos!

Joseph Goldstein writes (*Mindfulness: A Practical Guide to Awakening*, 386) regarding Right Action and Right Speech:

"What motivates and energizes us to make this effort are precisely the previous steps on the Path. As we understand through Right View the selfless, interconnected aspect of all things, and as we cultivate Right Thought of renunciation, loving kindness and compassion, then we are moved to speak and act in such a way that minimizes harm and is conducive to the welfare of all." Goldstein is teaching the Fourth Noble Truth, which is also known as the Eightfold Path. It is found in the teachings of the Buddha and is understood as the Path toward the end of suffering.

DELUSION AND FREEDOM

I was walking in a room with many windows.
I heard a light thump and looked up.
It was a tiny bird.
She was thumping against the very clean glass.
Five or six times she thumped.
Then she flew away to freedom.
How I wish the walls of delusion I meet in my mind could be
    released as well.
And then, this one, right here, could be free.

ENCOUNTER DURING THE GAZA WAR OF 2014

I am in Philadelphia. I am sitting across from a man who is
drinking mint tea. I am eating a salad with candied pecans and
blue cheese. We are in an upscale café in a gentrified area of the
city, where they serve gluten-free pizza and even advertise gluten-
free salad dressing.

The man is telling me about his car accident and his parents
who survived the Holocaust in Poland. He is near tears several
times. He knows I have just visited Lithuania and Israel. He
knows I went to Israel a couple of days before the Israeli army
invaded the Gaza Strip.

I start talking about the hardest few days of that trip. I had
traveled around Israel with a group of liberal American rabbis.
Ten of us had spent three days at the end of the trip, in the midst
of the war, in a place called Tantur. It is a beautiful pink stone
building surrounded by gardens, a hostel for Christian pilgrims
visiting the Holy Land. Tantur is situated on the Palestinian side
of the Green Line, Israel's 1967 border, and on the Israeli side
of the separation fence, wall, or barrier that surrounds the West
Bank. It overlooks Bethlehem and a very busy checkpoint where
Palestinian men cross over at 4:00 a.m. looking for work in Israel.
They return early, especially during the war, when there is no
work for them.

The ten of us American rabbis ranged in age from our mid-
thirties to late-sixties. I was the oldest. Our original trip had been
revised because of the war: Instead of visiting Bethlehem and
Hebron, we were staying at Tantur for three days, and the various

Palestinian speakers we were planning to meet were going to come speak to us. One after the other.

We met in a beautiful room with high ceilings and large open windows. The chairs were upholstered and very comfortable. There was tea, coffee, fruit, and pastries for snacking all day long. We had been instructed to listen and ask questions. We were a very agreeable and docile group; we know how to follow instructions. The staff was pleased that the speakers were still willing to come in the middle of the war. They were also pleased that the accommodations were so well appointed and comfortable and that the food was good.

A few weeks later when I am back in Philadelphia telling the man who is drinking mint tea about this experience, I realize that I am still very upset. In fact my body is still vibrating. I tell him I haven't been able to think about those three days without feeling terribly upset, that sometimes it feels like anger, but it is more likely grief, although I am not crying now. I tell him I'd cried while I was at Tantur, that, at night, in my room (I'd asked for a single and thankfully received one), I'd called Maynard, who was back home, and I'd wailed on the phone. I also tell the man that I'd cried in the small group when we were supposed to share our feelings with each other, but that I was not sure we were very supportive to each other. I say I thought we were all partially numb, overwhelmed, and confused. At least, I had been.

My lunch partner helps me understand what is going on for me. He said I'd never had so much hatred directed at me. Yes, it wasn't at me personally, but it was at Israel and the Jewish people, and I am part of that reality. I am part of the oppressor. He explains that these people are the ultimate and forever victims. Like the Jews used to be (and still sometimes feel they are). At moments, I'd recognize my deep kinship with these strangers: Indeed, they were not strangers at all. I felt responsible for holding their pain as I would hold my own. One after the other with personal sagas, with maps, with graphs, with large brown eyes, dressed in short skirts and jeans and wearing a jalabiyah. It was all the same. Some of them begged us as American Jews who were free to leave: "Tell your government about our suffering." The words kept being repeated: land, water, land, water, home, border crossing, police, prison, hatred, Israel, Israel, Israel. Yes, intentional.

At one point during those three days, it became impossible. I imagined putting a revolver to my own head. I felt I could not stand this anymore.

At lunch, back in Philadelphia, my companion tells me that this was as deep an experience of compassion or empathy that one could have—to sit still, to listen, to receive pure hatred, blame, abuse leveled at one's own kin, one's own soul, the structure of one's heart. It felt like I was drinking poison and could not digest it, could not swallow it, could not spit it out. Yet, I did not run away. Yes, I was, and still am, in pain, but I recognized that they were in worse pain. There was wisdom and generosity in them having been able to speak and in my having been able to hear. In that intersection separation was reduced. The speakers had thanked us deeply for being there. They'd thanked us for listening, for coming, for sitting still. They'd thanked us for overcoming the gulf of being a stranger.

While my companion drinks his tea, I explain how, adding to the stress, my colleagues in Tantur began to learn that their flights home were canceled. They called their travel agents and airlines while walking in and out of the sessions. I was sure that my flight would go because I had scheduled extra time on my "vacation" to hang with friends. Still, the drama of the situation did not escape me: the energy of being trapped, scrambling to get out, to get home. A paradox for Jews in their homeland. Where is the homeland? Where is my home? Where do any of us belong?

There is such a strong desire to make sense of this, to blame someone, or to fall into the abyss of shame. But I realize I must simply sit with the visceral vibrations of knowing this pain. Knowing that hatred and fear isolate and separate. Hatred and fear lead to war. But hatred and fear cannot easily be transformed. Hatred and fear corrode and solidify at the same time. They suck the lifeblood from my veins.

After Tantur, I had some sweet days with friends in Jerusalem. I spent a beautiful Sabbath in the city of golden light, delicious bread and cheeses, exquisite tomatoes and cucumbers, and endless gelato and frozen yogurt. My flight was canceled, but I arrived home only two days late. I dreamed about war every night for a week. Guilt and despair swirled in my mind, though by then I was far away.

It is so easy to be here now, in the upscale café, in the moment, to have the ability to put it aside, to be quiet, to rest, and not to know.

TIKKUN OLAM

Tikkun Olam has its origins in Jewish mysticism, magic, and theurgy. In contemporary circles it means social justice and is often translated as "to fix or repair the world."

Maybe tikkun is a bad term because to fix implies something is
    broken.
To heal is better; to hold is better yet ——
To hold the brokenness.
Let me hold my brokenness and from that almost unimaginable
    tenderness of course I will be able to hold yours.

IDRAH RABBAH

I wrote this poem after studying the Jewish mystical classic, the Zohar, with scholar Melila Hellner Eshed the winter after the Gaza war. Melila also shared a song that went viral in Israel after the war. It is based on a text from Rebbe Nachman of Bratslav and goes like this: "Even in the hiddenness that exists within the hiddenness, even here, divine awareness can be found." I based this poem on the Zohar text and a YouTube post of Israeli soldiers singing this song.

Two boys singing and a machine gun stands between them.
Two soldiers in green with a machine gun between them.
Young sweet boys.
One is playing a guitar.
Waiting, killing time.
Yes, it is urgent.
It is impossible.
And even in the urgent, impossible, unspeakable, utterly hidden,
    obscure, darkened shadow
Even here
We glimpse your radiant face.
In the taste that is not tasted
In the sound that is not heard
In the great gathering of words.
Words on a page.
Words spoken.
Lungs breathing words.
We pray.
We sing:

May the milk flow.
May the dew glisten in the orchard.
May the beast rest.
It is urgent.
We are talking about land, water, air, fire.
We are talking about children dying.
We are talking about talking about.

I WANTED MACARONI—
"WHEN THE LONGING CEASES, MY HEART STILLS."

I went to my eight-year-old granddaughter Hadassah's end-of-the-year chorus performance. I didn't understand the lyrics, and it was hard to hear the kids singing because the piano player was so loud, but, mercifully, it was not too long. After the "concert" they served potato chips, cookies, and pretzels. Five-year-old Yehuda moved quickly toward the food table after the applause. I noticed him stuffing his mouth with the goodies. He had at least three cookies and fistfuls of the salty snacks. The grown-ups were too distracted to set the usual limits: He took full advantage.

We had planned to go out to dinner at a new local restaurant with a veggie menu. We met there, and Yehuda's mom, Abby, ordered one grilled cheese sandwich with fries for both kids to share. She knew they wouldn't be very hungry after the snack fest.

But Yehuda was distressed. "I want macaroni," he proclaimed.

"You can share the grilled cheese with your sister," his mom replied. "I will make macaroni tomorrow night at home."

When the food arrived, the sandwich and the fries were divided between the kids. I poured a lake of ketchup on Yehuda's plate. He started dipping and eating the fries but would not touch his half of the grilled cheese.

During dinner he held his ground and avoided the grilled cheese diligently. He seemed happy eating the fries, but every so often he would grimace: His smooth, pink face turned pinker and scrunched up. He said in a whiny, annoyed, kind of miserable voice, "But I wanted the macaroni."

In that moment I could see he was suffering. I could see his craving; I could see his grasping; I could see his desire. I could see that his craving was his suffering. Then he would go back to eating the fries. The longing had ceased and his heart was still, until once again, he remembered he wanted the macaroni.

We suffer anywhere and anytime we insist that things be different than they are in this moment. This endless desire is the stranger in our hearts. Rather than prompt us to wise action, it locks us into a cycle of dissatisfaction and misery. It saps the energy of our aliveness. It makes us smaller.

THE SURPRISE

Harriet says I can use room 307 for spiritual direction. There is no key yet, but the Latino maintenance man is silently cordial about letting me into the room. It is a corner room with two sides that are just windows. So light. So beautiful. One window overlooks Broadway and one, West Fourth Street. There are soft-padded chairs, colorful paintings on the wall, and a small bookshelf. I see the name on the door—Adrienne Levine. I guess she is on sabbatical, which must be why I can use her room for these meetings. The room they gave me last year belonged to someone else on sabbatical. It had been incredibly messy. I had often felt tempted to straighten things up on the desk and the stacks on the floor and in the corners.

This room, however, is beautiful. I guess I lucked out. Maybe they think that since I see faculty members, I deserve a great room with two sides, just windows, a corner office. I accept the privilege. I remember back to when Maynard's sociology department moved to the new building and they gave him an office with a window, which he gave to one of his colleagues who was miserable because she didn't have one. He is so kind. He said, "The window isn't a big deal to me."

My new corner office is filled with light. I am in a great mood. Then I notice a photograph of Ace and Arnie, in fact, two photographs. One picture even has their kids in it. I recognize Ace and Arnie, of course, because I know them, but I don't know Adrienne. It strikes me odd that Adrienne has two photographs of Ace and Arnie in her office. Ace teaches Bible here, and I heard she was on sabbatical as well. I also see a few Bible textbooks on the shelf. I guess Adrienne must teach Bible too.

I see two students for spiritual direction. Then Judith comes in and says, "So cool, you are in this office. Oh right, Ace is on sabbatical."

"You mean Adrienne," I say.

"Yeah, everybody calls Adrienne Ace."

"Oh, of course," I say.

This reminds me of the time I was told not to drink anything caffeinated. I love black tea, especially strong tea like Irish breakfast. So, I bought a few boxes of decaffeinated Irish breakfast and had happily gone through one box already, thinking how great this tea was. Then I noticed it didn't say *decaffeinated* on the box. It was only in my mind. In my desire. In my sweet delusion.

This is what the mind does. It fills in. It makes up universes of alternate realities. Anyone who has ever sat in silent meditation knows this. The mind doesn't like not knowing what is going on, so it makes up things all the time. Stories can be harmless, like imagining that Ace and Adrienne are two different people. They can be a little more serious, like wishfully presuming the tea is decaf. Or the stories can be harmful and alienating—untrue assumptions about self and others that are limited and limiting. *These* stories keep us separate. *These* stories make us all into strangers.

GARRISON RETREAT CENTER FACES WEST POINT ACROSS THE HUDSON

Brown brick fortress
faces gray stone monolith
parted by a river
wide, grey and brown.
A river of tears.
On one side
in the stone house
men and women quell their fears by planning wars.
Fears multiply into fires.
On the other side
in the brick house
men and women sit in deep silence
touching their fears.
They soften and dissolve into light.

PART II

MINDFULNESS, MEDITATION, AND RETREAT PRACTICE

Mindfulness is non-judging awareness resting on what is happening in this moment. I think mindfulness is akin to God's loving the stranger. So much is going on in the human mind and heart. When we come into the present moment we wake up from a dream of "what just happened to me" and "what is going to happen next to me." We wake up from self-absorption; from being caught in the small, separate, unique self to the awareness that there is no one to whom this is happening. Life is happening. The present is the created world. God's universe. Just this. Now. There is no aversion, no preference, no craving something else, and no imagining something better or worse. There is just this. Call it God. Call it love. Pure awareness. No boundaries, no barriers. Just clear, expansive, unconfined. Open. There are many ways to create conditions that promote these moments. Contemplative practices intend to cultivate and sustain these moments. There are many ways to recognize and embrace God's love for the stranger that appears in this mind, this heart, this body.

SHAMOR V'ZACHOR IS MINDFULNESS

One verb
Three Hebrew letters
Shin—a rushing river
Mem—a primal hum
Reysh—a whispered roar
Shin-Mem reysh
Shamor
How to translate?
guarding
minding
keeping
observing
watching
caring for
protecting

being faithful,
being present,
paying attention.

setting an intention,
entering into a relationship,
embracing a value, a standard, a practice.

Shamor is a commitment to something greater than ourselves.

It is the effort to align with the whole.

It is the essence of the whole that is revealed in that alignment.

Then there is forgetting. We find ourselves doing something we did not plan to do or saying something we did not mean to say. Obstacles arise. There are excuses. We are tired, we are sick, we are held captive by our habits.

Then
becoming aware of being lost.
Knowing forgetfulness.
This is remembrance.
Zachor
returning again.
Zachor

Set a day aside to rest, allowing the mind to expand, the skin to be smooth. Guard this precious day. *Shomer Shabbat.*

Then forgetting about the Sabbath. Wandering. Straying. Until remembering again. We are back home.

In the Torah there are two versions of the Sabbath
   commandment.
Shamor in Exodus; *Zachor* in Deuteronomy.
Keep the Sabbath in Exodus,
Remember the Sabbath in Deuteronomy.
On Friday night we sing: *Shamor v'zachor b'dibbur echad.*
Shamor and *Zachor* are said in one word.
The two versions are one.
Shamor v'Zachor.
Be mindful and remember.

Knowing we are not mindful is a moment of remembering. In that moment of remembrance, there is a return. There is mindfulness. Remembering our intention is being present to our intention.

It is two. It is one.

Shomer HaBrit

Entering into a covenant with life itself.
Brit means compact, belonging, reciprocity, charter, contract,
agreement, and relationship.

It is a promise to love life. This promise keeps us alive.

Then there is forgetting, separation, loss of alignment.
Causing pain.
But the pain awakens and turns the part toward the whole
    (again); toward the *brit*.

Who is the *Shomer?*
Every effort to align with the whole.
Every white bone and bloody muscle doing its part.
All of us and each of us.

Shomer Yisrael
The Guardian of Israel
neither slumbers nor sleeps.

In any moment we can wake up.
It is we who are sleeping.
Wakefulness never sleeps.

Yisrael—
the spiritual wrestler—
finds refuge
in every moment,
in every breath,
in the warmth of the sun,
in the chill of the rain,
when the gate swings open,

when the door hinges close.
A strong arm as close as our shadow.

Shomer Mishpat

It is a lawful universe.

Shomer Mitzvot

Cultivating a peaceful heart.
Making the effort to align with something greater than ourselves.
Mitzvot are that effort.
Taking on a practice—Becoming *shomer mitzvot.*
Trying to connect.
With ourselves, each other, the past, the future, the whole thing.

Sacred longing arises—
to connect with the whole, to leave the separateness of this skin,
    to know luminosity at its source, to make space for the spa-
    ciousness—to heal, to serve, to praise, to know joy.

To know the center.
Multiplicity is released into unity.

Shomer Gerim–Adonai Shomer Et Gerim, Psalm 146:9

Adonai is mindful of strangers,
Immigrants, those under surveillance, from those places, the ones
    nobody knows, nobody talks to, the odd, the weird, the differ-
    ently abled,
With foreign accents, without family, without friends,
Without status, without protection, without regard, without
    homes, without insurance, without unions, without credit
    cards, without credentials.
Without documents.

Adonai keeps an eye on them all.

They are under God's watch.

Their destiny is God's concern

Their protection is God's business.

It is human work.

Shomer Adamah (Genesis 2:15)

In the garden, the human being is given the responsibility,
l'ovda u'l'shomra—to work the land and guard it.
Caring for the earth is an effort to align with something greater.

What does that mean?

If you care for something or someone, you pay attention when
   they are hurting.

You do not take away their gifts without knowing how to repay
   them.
You do not harm them.
You do not let others harm them.
You do not feed them poison.
You do not feed them garbage.
You honor their limits and appreciate their gifts.
You are careful with their life as if it were your own.
It is.

Hashomer Achi Anochi?

Am I my brother's *shomer?* Am I my brother's keeper?

How should I know where my brother is?
Is my brother my responsibility? Is my sister?

Why should I be concerned about his health, his work, her security, her children?

"I have my own troubles," says Cain.

Shomer Lashon

Guard your tongue.
Guard your tongue and lips, palate, teeth, windpipe, neck, lungs,
   and everything else involved in speaking.
Guard it all from lies, cruelty, and nonsense.
May we be willing to sit in silence rather than berate another
   with our words.

We welcome the gatekeeper, the one who restrains stories of
   malice, great and small, high-pitched rumors, smart-sounding
   judgments, mocking, sarcastic, slightly untrue repartee.

Shamor V'zachor b'dibur echad

Making an intention,
making an effort,
opening to what is greater, boundless, sacred, interwoven,
life.
Then forgetting.
Then realizing forgetfulness.
Rededicating. Returning. Remembering.
Bringing God into this place and this time.

Yivarechecha Adonai V'yishmerech

May Adonai,
Life, Reality, the Universe, the Mystery we call God,
be for you and me, all our loved ones, all our neighbors, all who
   share this earth with us,
a source of blessing and care, protection, ease and safety.

TIKKUN OLAM AS MINDFULNESS PRACTICE

Melanie was telling me about her experience of Rosh Hashanah. She felt that the meal was stuck in between other things. There wasn't enough time. And the parts she took in services were done in a breathless manner. Everything felt rushed, unsatisfying, jagged.

Where was the contentment, the celebration, the satisfaction? We stuff things in. Why? Because there is not enough time, and then we find we are not satisfied so we keep stuffing. We are breath less—literally with less breath, less life. Why? Because there is not enough time, so we stop breathing deeply. Does this satisfy us? Does this create more time?

Melanie's prayer is to realize what enough is. How does anyone know when it is enough? Enough breath, enough food, enough people, enough time, enough praise, enough activity, enough money, enough helping or being helped, enough progress, enough security, enough—Dai, daiyeinu!!

Are we not in a global crisis of what is enough? Is not the misallocation of resources a symptom of not knowing when enough is enough? Is not the oil crisis, the arms race, the crisis of credit, the excesses of obesity as well as anorexia a sign of the question unanswered—what is enough?

In order to address the macrocosmic questions, we need to have people who have confronted the microcosmic questions. We need to be simultaneously working on the inside and the outside. That is the contribution of spiritual practice to social change.

STRETCHING

Stretching
the back, the thighs, the belly, the jaw, the boundaries, the expectations, the acceptance, the fingers, the toes, the beliefs, the trust, the faith.

Opening
the heart, the hips, the knee creases, the eyes, the crevices between the toes, the mind, the willingness.

Touching
the floor, the ankles, him, her, everyone, everything—all the time. Being touched, grasping, holding, tousling, caressing, pushing, hugging, kissing.

Suspending
arms, head, feet, beliefs, fears. Dangling, swinging, hanging, swaying, swiveling.

Resting
the back, the bones, the muscles, the flesh, the hair follicles, the tongue, the throat, the hands, the arches of the feet, the thoughts, the head, the mind, the ideas—the soul.

Living Being
Loving Being
Discovering God.

THE SPIRITUALITY OF SILENCE

When Sylvia Boorstein and I cooked up the idea to bring rabbis on retreat to learn meditation and have them be in silence for four days, people thought we were crazy. "Are you kidding?" they exclaimed. "You think you are going to get rabbis or any Jews for that matter to be quiet for that long? It's not possible and, anyway, it's not Jewish!"

That was over twenty years ago. I have since had the pleasure of sitting in silence with many Jews—rabbis, cantors, educators, lay leaders—who have expressed gratitude for the opportunity. What is this all about?

Most important, it is about choosing to be silent. This is completely different than using silence as an instrument of power or punishment in a family or in a society. It is not "being silenced" or retreating into silence out of fear, confusion, or weakness. When we choose silence we set an intention to limit distraction and stimulation for a period of time. We create an oasis in the midst of the constant barrage of input in our lives. We create a Shabbat in the mind.

We establish conditions that help us see more clearly the way our minds work, the truth of this moment of experience. Silence is a structure that helps us cultivate awareness of what is happening in the moment. Silence helps us slow down and simplify in order to observe what is often obscured from view.

When we turn our awareness toward our own experience, we have a first-row view of how we suffer and struggle, what causes pain, and what leads to freedom. We recognize that suffering is the imperative of the mind insisting that things be different than what they are. In contemplative practice, we are our own laboratory, our own wisdom teacher. We see our habitual reactions. We hear the stories we have been telling ourselves forever. We become intimate with the rising and passing of all phenomena, with what is within our control and what is not. We learn in this very body what anger and fear feel like. We sense the inner landscape of generosity and peace. This learning stays with us when we return to conversation, sound, and speed. Silence is not the opposite of speech. It is a way to find the truths that need to be spoken, and a way of speaking them so that they can be heard. When we resume our lives, we have more tools to practice wise, true, and caring speech.

There are multiplicities of techniques that help cultivate awareness, just like there are many machines in the gym to build up our muscles. All of these practices are supported by a reduction of external stimuli. Their intention is to help us grow in freedom, wisdom, and love.

There are times when we enter the silence within the silence. We may be sitting and paying attention to what is arising and passing moment to moment. Suddenly boundaries may fall away and divisions may disappear. This is what we listen for when we say *Shma Yisrael*. We hope to enter the presence of the infinite, the eternal, and the mysterious, the presence of the One.

When we call upon *Yisrael* to "Listen" we are calling ourselves to wake up and show up. We are calling ourselves to know how deeply we are connected to each other, how we are not separate. We are calling ourselves to more wisdom, more love, and more peace. What could be a more Jewish practice?

ALLES IS GOTT IS MINDFULNESS

Alles is Gott.
That makes it simple.
Each spoonful of oats, raisins, and yogurt
touching this mouth, tongue, and teeth
filling this belly.
Right now.
Every cool breeze,
bird's song,
back pain.
Thought after thought.
Alles
Alles
Alles
Is Gott.

THE LIBERATION OF LAUGHTER

Life—on and off retreat—frequently confounds our expectations and undermines our illusion of control. Sometimes the direction is desirable and welcome; other times it is confounding and shocking. Humor breaks up the sense of the solidity of self. It doesn't take more than sitting with our own minds to see how crazy the mind is. Can we do anything else but laugh? The stuff we make up is funny. The things we look forward to: the food, the weather, the talk, going to sleep—walking when we are sitting and sitting when we are walking. It is funny. Whatever we think is going to be a certain way, it usually isn't. It's funny. One of the greatest things about the mind is its capacity to laugh—usually at itself. Indeed, the mind has a mind of its own!

My mother, Ida, was a very funny woman. She always enjoyed a good joke and a hearty laugh. When she was ninety-five she told one of her favorites: "An old guy runs into another old guy on the street. He gives him a look over and says: 'Tell me, Harry, who was it that just died, was it you or your brother?'"

In Jewish folklore, Chelm is a town of fools. It is a place where things never go smoothly despite the best intentions. In Chelm, there are always too many good ideas. It is a place where the obvious is obscure and the obscure is obvious—where great effort is expended, but results are unanticipated.

Whenever we hear a Chelm story we laugh at it. We are delighted by its antics. It is entertaining. Chelm is, of course, a giant mirror. We are looking at our own struggles and our own relationships. The laughter and self-recognition can be a healing balm to soothe our striving, our efforts at control and perfection. Humor has the power to embrace and caress our humanity like no other force in the world.

Chelm stories often speak about the strength of our ideas to keep us from seeing what is truly before us. Here is a good example. Once, while walking down the street in Chelm, a man stops another, greets him like an old friend, and embraces him with affection. "Isaac! Isaac!" the man says. "What has happened to you, Isaac? Such a long time I have not seen you. Look at yourself. How you have changed. You used to have a fine head of hair, thick like a mop. Now you have a bald head. What a change. Isaac! Isaac! What a man you were. You used to be strong like an ox with big, powerful shoulders. Look at you now, Isaac—small and shrunken, a nothing. Isaac—what a change! And your mustache, black and thick and shiny, shooting out from both sides like a sword. Ah, that was a mustache! Now, nothing but bare, pale skin. What a change! Isaac, Isaac, what has happened to you?"

"But I am not Isaac."

"Isaac, Isaac, so you have changed your name as well!"

It is fun to laugh at Chelm. But how many times is my life guided by mistaken impressions and fixed opinions that no dose of reality can or will contravene? Sometimes I am so sure I know the essence of another person, especially a person close to me, that I fail to listen to what she is saying. My unexamined fears and stories about life may cause me to be misled by rogues as easily as they cause me to miss out on friendship and tenderness. When I live in the past or in the future, I miss out on life. I live in Chelm. This is human. It happens all the time. We all do it. Can I embrace my own foibles with compassion and tenderness? Can Chelm help me accept in kindness and good humor all your pratfalls as well as my own?

One time I was sitting at a synagogue community meeting. I was the rabbi of the community. The meeting was going on and on. People were not making much sense to me. Everyone needed to say something. It was getting late. I was not sure what the topic was any more. Suddenly I understood. "This is Chelm." I was in Chelm. I relaxed and enjoyed the rest of the meeting.

The soul is called forth in laughter, in play, and in courage. The more that is revealed, the more freedom we have. Purim is a ribald, fun-house version of Passover. It comes at the end of winter. It celebrates a great reversal of the fortunes of the Jews in Persia from near annihilation to redemption. Like its season mate, Mardi Gras, it is a time of masks, costumes, and revelation through concealment. Purim is a celebration of shattered expectations and reversals. It calls forth qualities of heart and mind that help us navigate the waters of paradox and absurdity in order, ultimately, to see more broadly and more clearly. Near winter's end, nerves are frayed and the skies particularly unpredictable. It is a good time to make fun; to laugh—mostly at ourselves.

Another time, when I was on a silent retreat before the holiday of Purim, I was sitting for hours and hours in the meditation hall, aware of changing breath, sensations, and mind states. Suddenly, my mind filled with thoughts and images of an imagined character. The character is an Orthodox rabbi from Brooklyn, with sidelocks and a beard. The rabbi has a crazy sense of humor and is completely out of place in the progressive, egalitarian, gay-friendly Jewish Community of Amherst, Massachusetts. It strikes me very funny. I am so amused, I start laughing. I am sitting in the silent meditation hall trying desperately to control my own laughter. I get calm and then I hear another internal joke. It starts again. This is the experience everyone has had thinking something ridiculously funny at a somber moment—at a funeral, for instance. For the Purim celebration at the synagogue I decide to come as the Orthodox bearded rabbi. What will be revealed in this concealment?

MEDITATION IS A NARROW BRIDGE

Taking a moment to breathe—a few conscious inhales and
   exhales.
Now pausing after the third or fourth exhale and waiting.
Waiting for the breath to arise.
Waiting to be breathed.
Noticing any effort to pull the breath toward you.

Just waiting to be breathed.

Letting inhale turn into exhale.
Waiting again. Receiving. Being breathed.
Resting in the miracle of this breath.

Today.
Now.
Again and again.
Resting with confidence
in the Divine breathing.

HERE IS A LIST OF MANTRAS

It's okay
It's just . . .
What is here?
Befriending yourself
Underdoing
Good enough
Starting from where you are
Trusting the path
I love you, keep going
Nowhere to go, nothing to do, no one to be
Letting the retreat do you
Allowing dissolving to happen
Being alive is enough
No experience to have
Nothing to figure out
This is like this
Letting go
Letting be
Nothing has to happen
There is nothing to do
Trusting emergence
Ease
Shhh . . .
There, there, sweetheart

CAN I FORGIVE MYSELF?

Can I forgive myself?
For striving, for preaching peace and mostly being at war,
War, with time, with my body, yes, even with dear friends whose
     standard I try to match.
Can I forgive myself for not knowing how to rest?
Although we would all say the Sabbath is the holiest day.
Can I forgive myself for trying to predict and arrange the future
     so I can be safe even though I know there is only one true
     source of safety?
Can I forgive myself for trying to take care of everything, as if I
     could?
Can I forgive myself for the rewards I have gained from
     striving—
The praise, recognition, and admiration?
Can I forgive myself?
Old feminist, post-holocaust, third-generation, middle-class Jew
     living at the end of the American empire?
Can I say, "Ok, you did great and now it is time to turn, to turn
     slowly and sit down, without an agenda, without a clue."
Just like that.
Getting close to life before it is over.
There really is no one to forgive us, is there?
Just stardust making its way home.

POEMS WRITTEN ON A SILENT RETREAT

While the meditation instruction is to let the mind rest, it is usual to notice the fountain of fragmentary words, thoughts, stories, images, and conversations that gush forth. These poems chart some of these fragments, the feelings and association that seemingly spring from nowhere. Sometimes, wisdom emerges from awareness of these arisings.

One: Tonight I made a mistake.

I served the shepherd's pie.

I took it out of the oven and put it on the table and shut the oven off.

Then the cook came in.

Disapproving.

She hadn't checked to see if it was hot—all the way through (it was a leftover).

I read disapproval in her eyes, her lips, in her hands, in the tilt of her head.

And disapproval went through me.

I defended myself: "Well," I said, "I didn't know anyone was coming and I saw the note that said 'shepherd's pie' at my work table and I figured . . ."

She was not going to yield.

Okay.

I felt the tears come to my eyes and the thought, This is ridiculous. This is no big deal.

I few tears leaked out when I went to the bathroom.

Then I got my tea.

Oh, first she asked me to take a scoop of shepherd's pie from the
   middle of the pan and see if it was hot.
I did it.
It was warm.
"Okay, leave it," the cook said.
I took a rice cake and my hard-boiled egg from breakfast and
   some slices of pear and apple and my tea—Ceylon decaf.
When I sat down to eat I mused about the pain.
What it's like to make a mistake and have serious consequences.
Yes, I know someone who did that once.
My mother wasn't watching once.
A pain like that could consume a life.

Two: Swirling thoughts,
Dots of clarity, blotches of confusion.
Lights go on and off.
It's raining now.
I want something. Anything.
Anything, but this.

Three: Surrender.
Now there's a word that contradicts everything I have ever
   learned.
But it's not about giving up forever or being like a sheep led to
   slaughter—the Lord is my shepherd—forget about it.
No.
Surrender to this moment.
Just let it be without desire to make it different.
A moment of pure existence that rises like a bubble from a bowl
   of suds.
A moment free of needing to make it this or that.
Just a leaf falling now.
A sadness in the heart.

A sore knee.
A clear note.

Four: Sitting in the hall which is so quiet and the halls are so
    quiet and I feel large and noisy and clumsy.
Sitting with that familiar feeling of taking up too much space,
    wanting to be tinier, more delicate, more quiet.
Not to disturb.
Not to annoy my parents—
Tears come, hot ones—
In the hall.
And I will make noise if I raise my hand with a tissue.
And I am flooded with family scenes and feeling too big and
    invisible at the same time.
Thanksgiving and Passover.
Passover and Thanksgiving.
And more tears and sounds.
And then it's quiet.

*Five: In a practice interview on one long retreat, I spoke with a
teacher about my effort to teach the dharma to the Jews, in a Jewish
language. She said, "You are holding up a pole." That is how this poem
emerged.*

You said I am holding up a pole.
A curious expression.
I know you were thinking of teaching dharma in Jewish.
But which pole did you mean?
Was it a fishing pole looking for salmon in the icy river or a tent
    pole ?
Holding up a shelter in the wind? Or the North or South Pole?
Was it the pole one vaults or the poll one takes by asking ques-
    tions or is it where you press levers and hope for the best?

Did you mean I was holding up the flagpole—and what flag do I
    fly, if any?
I think you meant something hard to grasp.
Perhaps, though, my pole is one of magnetic force or maybe it's
    the striped one that tells me I have found the barber.
Or maybe it's the opposite pole to all the messages of the culture
    or the religion or the market.
Or maybe it's a chupah pole holding up the canopy where bride
    and groom will stand and drink the wine of blessing.
So, I stand, hand on the pole—be it plastic, wood, or metal—
    a phrase, a word—a suggestion so that I would not feel so
    lonely.

Six: The desire to get it right, do it right, have the right
    experience
And seeing how impossible this is
Because nothing lasts and the ground keeps moving
And that is the way it is.
The desire arises to just try harder
Or get a better technique, teaching, teacher, doctor, therapist,
    drug, thought, book, anything, anything that will make this
    discontent go away.
And the desires and discontents are all centered around a
    mirage—me.
A constellation of forces coming in and out.
Who did you say is trying to attain perfection, which is not
    attainable anyway?
Judgment,
Desire, control, planning, fixing, comparing, desire, fantasy, future,
    past—all experience is not reliable.
Not reliable.
Do you hear?
So, from this clear seeing, one worthy thing can be born.

We can call it faith.
But not faith to preach or broadcast or bank.
Faith to be here in this true place, right now.
Faith to open, allow, and sing letting the air go through
   unobstructed.
Faith to stretch the toes and fingers to the bone—
To unfold the wings—
To fly.
And then do it again.

Seven: I am awakened to the morning star—bright Venus in a sky
   just about to brighten.
Palest blue now and she is a disappearing memory,
light orange incandescent rising as a backdrop to the trees.
Changing, changing, changing.
Moment to moment as the earth puts on lights and shadows.
As the morning star disappears in the lightness,
as the treeless leaves greet the leafless trees,
as I get ready to walk to breakfast,
taking this newly born body to the first feast,
opening to the lights and shadows, now dancing, now resting,
   knowing they will soon disappear again.

THE MONTH OF JUNE

My deepening understanding of the ephemeral passing of experience helps me be more present for celebrations as well as the times of loss and mourning. The ephemeral unites friend and stranger, known and unknown, now and then. All dichotomies dissolve when we behold the passing of time.

There are some months of the year
when we can pretend things don't change.
Maybe February is a month like that.
Not much happens then.
But in June, we wave goodbye in loose black robes,
change our rooms, our names, our states.
We walk across thresholds smiling and sobbing.
June is the time of sendoffs, toasts, making memories,
sharing teary hugs as we stand on sandy toes in the moonlight.
June is the time of endings that appear to be beginnings but we
    know we are not really going to roll the scroll back to Genesis.
They are endings.
But they are beginnings too,
for every fruit cradles a seed and every crushed brown leaf feeds
    the soil of birth.

NIAGARA FALLS

It is poignant to recall that our experiences change when viewed from afar.

Flying from Hartford to Detroit
Thirty seven thousand feet above the earth
The flight attendant says, "There will be a great view of Niagara
    Falls on the right."
I am sitting in a window seat.
I remember when we drove to Wisconsin from Massachusetts
    and stopped to see the Falls. I said to Maynard, "This is one
    thing that is not overrated."
Now I look down.
I see squares of brown, green, and a blue ribbon of water.
The flight attendant is wearing jack o' lantern earrings and a Hal-
    loween vest.
She says, "It looks like a wisp of smoke."
I see a one-inch column of white. So small. I see a few white lines
    etched on the blue ribbon.
Is that it? I think to myself.
I ask the man in the plaid shirt and jeans sitting next to me if he
    wants to see it.
"I'll move out of the way," I say.
He stretches past me to look.
"Wow, it's so tiny I never would have noticed it," I say to him.
"Yeah, the Grand Canyon is like that too from an airplane."
I look again and the white smudge is in the right corner of my
    window. I crane my neck. It doesn't move. Soon it is gone.

EMPTY

What is the secret of aging well? Wise Aging? I know one thing—it's not obvious or easy.

How do I love this changing body?
I do not want to lose what I have.
I do not want to get old.
I do not want to die.

The antidote?
I am not I.
I am not separate from this.
I am an arising and a passing, a wave, a cloud, a snowflake.

But wait. What about the mind that denies this?
What about a mind that does not trust what brings freedom and
    peace?
Ahhhh!!! What a predicament.
What a practice!
Take an indelible pen and mark Empty on my soul. Empty.
    On the soles of my feet.
When I walk or dance, the truth of Empty will bounce me to
    the sky.

HAIKU

See the star on the stage
incandescent and evaporating
each moment.

Arising and dissolving,
nothing personal.
The breath and the tree.

Green bamboo brown bamboo,
tree to log to wood chip.
All is one.

Brown spots,
brown leaves,
dry earth powder.

Sitting in a graveyard.
Nothing to do but
be a little kinder.

Sky was so blue.
Now wispy clouds cross it.
Still the sun shines through.

PRAYING IN TRANSITION

The transition in my life from full-time to part-time work and toward retirement and old age is reflected in the season. It is a dappled time. It is a golden time. The earth's process interweaves with my reflections and prayers. What are your transitions? What are your prayers?

Golden sunshine,
bright golden leaves
nearly blinding.

I pray for acceptance and wisdom, deeply wanting to give myself away, but in a different way. I pray to enjoy life, feel nurtured, and truly embrace the love in my life.

Dappled dry leaves
crunching under my foot:
I stop and kiss the ground.

I pray that the spiritual awareness I have unearthed be realized fully so it can serve as a beacon, a witness to God and others—a witness to my purpose and my legacy.

The oldest tree in Pennsylvania
embraces me;
We have one mother.

And there are challenges—like strength and energy and especially balance. Also just remembering. And getting so tired. And habitual striving. Habitual good girl. And the next new pain that shows up in the body and wants my attention. And fear is still here.

Amazing standing log,
upright on three legs.
A face but no roots.

Dreaming again.
Wanting solace,
there's only change.

Roots, yes, I have them. Some are crumbling, being questioned. Still I have Torah, Jewish community, the world of mysticism, wisdom literature, poetry, music. There is so much to draw upon. No reason to despair.

Many trees with split trunks
divided in two.
How well I know.

In many ways less divided now, clearer, knowing when to say yes and no, not needing a face anymore, not wanting to appear as anything or anyone. The time is urgent. The tasks are immense. I pray to recall to call upon the Source of All.

Every leaf and nut
knows it is the season
to return in love.

Returning to the Source of faith and love. What else gave birth to everything and what else awaits us at the end? Miracle of miracles. No matter who you are.

Super large magnolia leaves
fallen, dried and brown.
Size no safe haven.

Neither size nor accomplishment, brilliance, cleverness, wit, not even friendliness, lovability.
We all return to the earth like the leaves in autumn.

And there still is plenty to unfold, perhaps. Who knows? Staying open. New teachers, new friends, new students, children, learning . . . New struggles, new campaigns, losses and victories—who knows?

Delicate mini oak leaves
Still perfectly green
This time of year.

KUAN YIN SHECHINAH

Kuan Yin *is the incarnation of compassion in Buddhism.* Shechinah *is the female aspect of Divinity, mother, healer, and earth.*

She doesn't want me to be good.
She just wants me to be happy.
She doesn't need me to be safe.
She just wants me to trust.
She doesn't care if I am the best, because there are no superlatives
    in her vocabulary.
All her words are already perfect, still, and whole.
They dissolve into space, not taking up any room.
They are without movement or preference or sound.

SNOW FALLING ON SNOW

Sylvia gave me the suggestion in this poem when I went on a six-week silent retreat. I suspect the implied instruction was to allow a spacious mind to unfold, a mind that is not fighting with reality, not creating suffering, not insisting that things be a certain way. Rather, she wanted me to recognize that when I can look at something with clear comprehension, not demanding it be different than what it is, then, kindness and compassion may arise.

My friend said, "Think of me when
You hear snow falling on snow."
Well, I have thought of you, dear friend, quite a bit.
But I haven't been able to hear snow falling on snow.
Oh, we have had plenty of snow—
Luscious, white, luxurious snow—
Plenty of snow falling on snow.
And I have tried to hear the sound.
I thought maybe my hearing is not so good.
Or maybe, I am not trying hard enough.
I even knelt down and put my ear to the ground.
Silence.
And I thought of my friend and smiled.
Maybe it's a koan.
Could be.
She is a Buddhist.
A Jew, too.
Sort of like, "What's the sound of one hand clapping?"
Listen to the sound of snow falling on snow.

Just listen
Just
Listen
And fall into
The emptiness
The luminescence
The everlasting.

WINTER

Winter light has
color but so little warmth.
Catching sunrise and sunset
these days.
Mauve orange and peach blush,
lipstick names,
beautiful and shallow.
Not touching the inside
which stays cool, cold, frozen, numb.

Say it!
It is so.
The winter sun
is under the snow.

YERIDA TZORECH ALIYAH—FALLDOWNGETUP

Here are two Hasidic teachings (translated by Rabbi Jonathan Slater) that articulate a contemplative approach to the human condition.

A Text Attributed to the Baal Shem Tov Tzava'at HaRIVa"Sh #64: "Sometimes we may fall from our developed spiritual state due to our own needs, since God may know that we need this. Other times, other people may cause us to fall from this state. But, this descent is for the sake of our later, higher ascent, as in the verse: 'He will lead us over and beyond death *(al mut)'* (Psalms 48:15). Further we read: 'Abram descended into Egypt' (Genesis 12:10) and 'Abram came up out of Egypt' (Genesis 13:1). 'Abram' is the soul, and 'Egypt' is the husk."

A Text from the Hasidic Master Degel Macheneh Efraim on Vayetze: "'Jacob left Beer-sheba, and set out for Haran. He came upon a certain place [and stopped there for the night, for the sun had set]. He took one of the stones of that place. [He put it under his head and lay down in that place. He had a dream:] a ladder was set on the ground and its top reached to the sky, and angels of God were going up and down on it' (Genesis 28:10:12). In these verses we find the mystery of expanded and contracted consciousness, as explicated by my sainted grandfather (the Baal Shem Tov): 'The *chiyyut* [life force] moves away and comes back' (Ezekiel 1:14), and it is impossible to remain on one spiritual level for all time. Rather, we go up and down, and the descent is for the sake of later ascent. When we are finally able to recognize, to know and feel this contracted state, and pray to God—along the lines of 'But if you search from that place for YHVH your God, you will find Him, [if only you seek Him with all your heart and soul]' (Deuteronomy 4:29)—from that place, the spiritual state in which we find ourselves."

I recognize that times of constriction are not separate from times of expansion. I realize that, when I bring an attitude of mindfulness toward the ebb and flow of life, life does what it does, namely ebbs and flows. Indeed, I see that my reluctance to embrace the moments of apparent darkening actually blocks the natural flow of darkness into light.

I see in my mind and body the desire to cling to the pleasant and avoid the unpleasant. Everybody does this. This is useful wiring. It is important for my survival. However, when I act only out of habit and reactivity and always push away or run away from the unpleasant, I limit my freedom and growth as a conscious being.

I am cultivating, through mindful awareness of this moment, without judgment, the capacity to choose more wisely. I am cultivating the capacity to be with the down slide, the *yerida,* and see that, as I bring my full attention to this moment, the veils lift. Down is revealed as a ramp for Up. Patient attention to the fog allows the sun's magnificence to be perceived. It is the ability to be here, to be still, to enter the spaces, the unknown in-between, that nourishes the spiral of growth.

Following are seven attitudes I seek to cultivate to bring to the *yerida* moments, the times of confusion, contraction, alienation, exile:

Patience. Being with what is right now and knowing that I am not able to change it, I breathe into this moment. I offer myself an attitude of kindness toward thoughts of blame or anger that may arise. I notice the experience of impatience in my body.

I am practicing patience by being with a moment that I am not able to change or control. There are ample opportunities in life to practice this quality, such as when I am on the slowest line in the supermarket while all the other lines are longer, or when the computer is not responding, or when my husband is taking forever to get ready when we are already late. If I use my descent into impatience and irritability skillfully, I might discover an enhancement of the pleasant, relaxed, and useful quality of patience in my life.

This is the practice,
This is how the heart gets purified,
This is how we get to know God.
Again and again and again—
Ill at ease
Distant
Separate
Uncomfortable
Critical thoughts of self and other
Race in the mind,
Inadequate, not quite okay, just off-center
Like mice in a maze.
The mind is the
Mice and the maze.
Again and again,
Until a moment of—oh, yes—
This is suffering!
Relentless, underground,
And again and again and again,
It is protecting something,
Which turns out invariably
To be "ME".
Then comes the grace, the mindfulness, the compassion.

Warm attention to the frozen and contracted, tender light on the shadows of delusion.

And then a moment of freedom.

Relax the heart.

You are home.

Empty

    Happy

One.

Decentering the "I": Moving into the passive voice. When in a *yerida* moment, the mind has a tendency to fabricate messages that often begin with the first-person pronoun: "I am angry"; "I am not a good meditator or person or friend or parent"; "I am hot, uncomfortable, sleepy etc."; "I have a pain in my knee, hip, lower back, shoulder, neck." Notice this and name what is arising while putting it into the passive voice. It is just happening. This is not about any "I" doing any thing. "Angry feelings are known now"; "Negative thought patterns are known now"; "Heat, discomfort, sleepiness are known now." "Unpleasant sensations in the knee, hip, lower back, shoulder, and neck are known now." Investigating what it feels like to move away from an identity of self allows me to see transience. It is an extraordinary revelation to see that clutching the "I" as the great doer, feeler, and thinker *is* the arising of suffering. Seeing constriction, whether it is a mind state such as anger, a physical pain, or a story of resentment or blame as conditions that are known in this moment, can relieve and diminish suffering.

Moving into Mystery. When I am in a *yerida* moment, I get scared. I am afraid things will never change, even though I surely know things always change. In an attempt to master this fear, I often tell stories and make up explanations that confuse me further. I am more skillful when I notice contraction of any kind and am willing to let go of explanation and analysis. In an airplane for instance, the mind might begin to interpret a bump as a sure sign of imminent danger. The truth is I have no idea what that bump means as I know nothing about aviation. Instead I might move into the mystery and ask the question: "What is this?" This is an experiential rather than an intellectual question. This is a question to the body. What is going on right now? This openness allows the pulsation of life to move freely. I might realize that my imaginary explanation is feeding my anxiety and keeping it from moving through as the passing state, which it is.

Ezah Hu Chacham? Lomed Me Kol Echad: Who is wise? He is the one who learns from everyone. This radical teaching encourages investigation and curiosity, without judgment and without attachment. Wisdom is a living process. It is an exploration of our lives. Wisdom entails a willingness to get close and intimate, even with moments that are painful and confused. It requires learning from all the teachers, those who make the best appearance, and those who we would rather never have come into our lives. *Kol Echad* means everyone—without exception, especially the stranger. In the Jewish mystical text the *Zohar*, the greatest insights emerge from the mouths of donkey drivers, old men, young children, and hermits in the desert. We usually are not told their names. What would it be like to go through life with such a learning attitude? Some days there are substitutes or new teachers in the yoga studio where I practice. Sometimes they are not to my liking for whatever reason—tone of voice, style, face, you name it. If my goal in life is to develop wisdom, most of my preferences and opinions are superficial. I embrace the fact that I can practice yoga and, indeed, learn from every teacher. Every moment has the potential to make me free.

Humor. We are back in Chelm. Or we have never left. Humor is the great tool of those on the bottom; hence it works well when we are going downhill—*yerida*. Humor overturns the carts of oppression. Humor is an automatic releaser of tension, a loosening of the belt that confines us to our habits and concepts. If I sit for any amount of time with the contents of my mind, the thoughts that arise willy-nilly, I simply have to laugh. The laughter lightens me up and allows the transformation to occur. It is another way to release the frozen breath and reenter the flow of life.

Gratitude. All prayers are drenched in gratitude. Those who pray know the secret that gratitude is the great transformer. How can I stay stuck and grateful at the same time? It's not possible. Gratitude opens the heart and connects me to the simple and the amazing. Gratitude cuts the ego down to size. Who, after all, is responsible for my ability to see the golden tree this afternoon, or feel the cool sweetness of the breeze, or have a meal that satisfies me, or a sweater that keeps me warm? Whom can I thank for being able to move my fingers and toes, for this breath, this breath, this breath? The downward spiral of my neediness dissolves in the bliss of gratitude.

The Collective. Sometimes I cannot connect to any of the above or any of the other skillful tools that help lift me or remind me that my life is not permanently stuck on the down dial. Sometimes, maybe often, I cannot lift myself up. But you—my friend, my teacher, comrade, colleague, fellow seeker—you can. I call out and you answer. You remind me that I am not always like this. You remind me that I have had other moments, and I will again. You remind me that this happened before . . . and *remember?* In your presence, I am no longer alone. I am no longer separate. The very exchange of our breath reminds me that my borders are far more permeable than I suppose.

We each have our own path.
That very thought cuts through comparing, judgment, checking
in every other second, "Am I doing it right?"

God is here! And here I am!

Hineni!

Like every brown leaf or forest mushroom or rock is completely
unique

I have never been and never will be again and have no idea what
needs to unfold.

And yet we gather together and speak languages and celebrate
and hold each other and know we are all going thorough the
same thing and share the same destiny.

PART III

GOD LOVES
THE STRANGER

In this section we move our attention from our inner world to the outer world. In both dimensions we encounter limited ideas and impressions that impede our happiness and ease. We recall that each time we meet a stranger, we look into a mirror at our own fears, longings, and hopes. Perhaps this is why the stranger is such a big theme in the Torah.

Toward the end of Leviticus and the Holiness Code, the Torah is concerned with ritual boundaries and rules. Specific instructions for the purity and eligibility of priests, and the requirements for the sacrificial offerings, are transmitted. Regulations for the Sabbath and annual festivals, and for the maintenance of the lamp and display bread in the portable sanctuary are proclaimed.

Meanwhile, a thin thread runs through both the narrative and the laws. It is a reference to the *ger*, the stranger, the immigrant, or the convert: the perennial "other." This is a huge preoccupation of Torah. The Israelites have experienced persecution as the hated and dreaded foreign element in Egyptian society, and their primary mandate as a free people is not to oppress the stranger. In the heart of the priestly holiness code, these words appear: "When a stranger resides with you in your land, you shall not wrong him. The stranger who resides with you shall be to you as one of your citizens; you shall love him as yourself, for you were strangers in the land of Egypt; I am the Lord your God" (Leviticus 19:33–34).

Deep in these accounts of arcane ritual details, the *ger* is referenced. Perhaps it is not surprising that in establishing rubrics and norms for who presides over important community functions and how those rites work, the question, "Who is in the community and who is not" rears its head. This is a human preoccupation. It begins when we are little and a new kid comes to school. Is she going to be included in our group? What if he isn't the same as us? What if she has another color skin or an accent or wears different clothes? We may not feel safe including the other in our games, our secrets, and our confidence. We may fear that he or she will take away the attention of the teacher or the wordless understandings we have built up with those in our own group.

We engage a similar anxiety in determining political policy. The United States has always been a nation of immigrants, a nation of strangers. But what is a just and compassionate immigration system? What would a wise, humane, and effective security policy look like? As I write these words in the months leading to the 2016 Presidential election, after the massacre in Orlando, the nation is preoccupied with the "stranger." In my heart, I wonder how a sense of safety can be established. I believe that hatred only increases hatred. How can I embody that truth? How can I bring compassion to my own discomfort and to the discomfort of others?

The Torah's strongest instruction is never to do to the *ger*, the stranger, the other, what was done to the Israelites by the Egyptians. It intends to break the compulsive repetition cycle in which the abused becomes the abuser. This is the dominant motif. According to Rabbi Eliezer in the Talmud (Baba Metsia 59b), the Torah "warns against the wrongdoing of a *ger* in thirty-six places; others say in forty-six places."

In the middle of the Torah account of the holiday cycle replete with details about observance and sacrifices it says: "And when you reap the harvest of your land, you shall not reap all the way to the edges of your field or gather the gleanings of your harvest; you shall leave them for the poor and the stranger: I YHWH am your God" (Leviticus 23:22). This is a radical juxtaposition. In the midst of the ritual celebration of the harvest, an economic program that includes the stranger is installed. The source of the caring for the poor and the stranger is the same. It is the life force itself, the source of all that proclaims justice and love.

THE SHOFAR AND THE TEARS OF OUR MOTHERS

We begin our Jewish year on Rosh Hashanah by listening attentively to hear shofar sounds. We conclude the Day of Atonement, the holiest day of the year, with a shofar blast. Jewish tradition equates the sound of the shofar with the cries of mothers: The mother of Israel's enemy Sisera and the wailing of the mother of Israel, Sarah, are both represented in the sounds of the shofar. Mothers' tears, filled with love, filled with grief, contain every conflicting emotion in the human soul. It doesn't matter if these mothers are friends or enemies. Their pain knows no borders. It is the pain of the mother of us all, this Earth, as the glaciers melt into her tears. It is a feeling of compassion, for the mother knows no divisions and no judgments and no politics. We are not asked to resolve anything. We are asked to open to hear the pain, whether it is the pain of our own lives or the pain of the other; the pain of our enemy or friend; the pain of our tribe or the pain of the world. No matter. It is all pain; it is as wordless as the shofar and as raw. It is a series of oscillating cries—whole, broken, shattered, and whole again. It is our practice. Being with the pain, the sound—only this sound—as it reverberates in our own skin and the skin of the world. This is the healing work that engages us. It takes everything from us, and what does it ask? Most of all it asks us just to be near, to be quiet, to stand, to sit, to walk, to eat, to sleep—in kindness, faithfulness, and peace. We dedicate our practice to all who suffer in this world of endless beauty and glory. May the shofar blast of all the cries of all the mothers and fathers, sisters and brothers awaken itself to the Source of Compassion that awakens the world to compassion.

THE KINDNESS OF STRANGERS

Kindness is a theme of Shabbat. The spaciousness and altered time sustains and supports the choice of kindness. The essence of the one we worship is kindness. The one thing we know that is not truly impermanent, that survives death, that beckons immortality, is kindness. The proof is in Psalm 136, which has as its refrain *kee l'olam chasdo*—for loving-kindness is eternal.

On Shabbat we have more time for practice. Prayer practice is a way to sweeten the mind and develop wisdom. Words create a sense of fullness that is beyond the mind's ability to grasp or hold. A beautiful example of expansive prayer on Shabbat is the *Nishmat Kol Chai*. "We could not thank you enough for even one of the thousand thousands and myriad of myriad favors . . . all our innermost being sings praises." The breath is so deep. The soul is free and soaring. Words pale.

The Torah commandment calling us to remember the Sabbath, surprisingly includes the stranger (Exodus 20:10): The kindness of the Sabbath includes the stranger in our midst. In other words, there really is no stranger when it comes to the depth of wishing our fellow creatures well.

Recently, I had two small and enormous experiences of kindness and strangers. Rabbi Jeff Roth, my dear friend and meditation co-teacher, and I were invited by a Japanese Buddhist group, Shin yo en, to visit Japan and be part of a pilgrimage to holy Buddhist and Shinto sites and an interfaith contemplative dialogue with a small group of Christians, Moslems, Hindus, and Buddhists. Jeff and I were the only Jews. It was fabulous. The hospitality was legendary. The food was incredible. The beauty was overwhelming. I was especially moved by the careful attention to detail, to the aura of mindfulness, kind and loving awareness moment to moment. The last day Jeff and I went shopping in Kyoto before getting our plane in Osaka, about two hours away by bus. A driver and another man accompanying the trip brought us into town and told us we could store our luggage at the bus station while we shopped. It turned out that all of the luggage checking areas were full. It was a Japanese holiday and Kyoto was filled with vacationers. The man who had accompanied us said, "No worries. I will stay with your luggage for a few hours while you shop. I will sit in a café and guard it." This was the gist of what he said in translated Japanese. We agreed. When we returned he greeted us warmly. I smiled in return. He had been so kind: He had given of his time to just sit there while he offered us the generosity of not having to schlep our heavy suitcases from store to store, shopping for souvenirs. It would never have occurred to me to ask this favor, and yet it arose in him spontaneously. It was so simple and yet a warm and beautiful act. He also waited for us as we left on a bus for the airport. He waved as the bus took off. I don't know this man's name, but I do believe I will remember him for a very long time.

Before this trip my primary impressions of Japan came from sushi, from owning a Toyota, from having photos of Hiroshima and Nagasaki etched in my brain, and from a story by Barbara Kingsolver titled: *Going to Japan*. In that story she describes the exquisite politeness of the Japanese. The Japanese language, in fact, she explains, does not accommodate insults, only infinite degrees of apology. What I came to appreciate from this short trip was how good it had felt to be treated with such kindness. How I had relaxed and become happier, and how I'd wanted to reciprocate. It was calming for my nervous system as well to have never seen litter in the streets or subways. I was comforted by perceiving these acts of devotion coupled with the beauty and symmetry created by gardeners in the public parks as they attentively trimmed each pine needle cluster so they would point up to the heavens.

A few weeks later, on my way from Philadelphia to Los Angeles with Maynard, I had another encounter with kindness. For some reason the airline had put us both in middle seats in one row behind the other. We asked for new seats, but, of course, the plane was filled to capacity. Despite the fact that we had booked together, we didn't have the clout to get two seats together. I was angry. As we were moving toward our seats, a woman sitting on the aisle watched as we tried to organize ourselves. Then she spontaneously offered to swap her aisle seat for the middle seat in the other row so we could sit together. I was so touched. She was a complete stranger. It was an act of kindness that melted the separation, that healed any ill will, that liberated my heart and mind. I trust that her generosity had given her a feeling of happiness, and that she knew her kindness was appreciated and received in gratitude.

Another story: It was Martin Luther King Jr.'s birthday in January 2015, a year of emerging awareness that racism in the United States is both deeply rooted and unacknowledged. I went with my daughter and her kids to a MLK Day and "Black Lives Matter" march and rally in Philadelphia. Hadassah, eight-and-a-half-years-old, listened closely to the speakers. Then she asked me: "Grandma, if the black people have been hurt so badly and are so angry and they get power, will they do to the whites what the whites did to them?" I said, "Great question, honey. That is why in the Torah it specifically says: 'You shall love the stranger because you were strangers in the land of Egypt.' That means we should not let fear and revenge take over. Even though we may have been hurt, we need to love those who are hurting."

The concentrated mind is a gateway to wisdom, non-separation, and love.

KEUR IBRAH FALL, SENEGAL

A few years ago I had the opportunity to be a stranger in a strange land. I went to Senegal as a scholar on a service and learning project of young rabbis. The American Jewish World Service (AJWS) organized the trip; our main base was in a rural town called Keur Ibrah Fall. Following is an account of a couple of particularly memorable experiences I had while I was there.

A young girl, fifteen, takes my hand and leads me to her house. "Baila" she says. Baila means dance in Spanish, a language I do understand, but she is speaking Wolof. She hands me a broom made out of sticks—it doesn't have a handle. I realize that Baila means "sweep" in Wolof. The girl motions to me in a gesture and says, "Sweep my house." Then I imagine the translation of the stream of words in Wolof: "I live here with my parents and seven or eight brothers. You came to help. We need the house to be cleaned so get started. I will show you how." She has the smooth skin of youth, the color of bittersweet chocolate. She wears an orange nylon t-shirt and a long cotton skirt with swirling lines of green and blue. It is tied at her waist. No shoes.

I take the broom and start to sweep. She frowns and shows me again. "Use the side of the twigs," she says in what I am guessing in Wolof. She is moderately impatient with me. I smile weakly and try again.

The floor is made of dirt that has been plastered over. There are a lot of holes and cracks where sand collects. It is Senegal, the

Sahel, where the soil is always dry. Dust is everywhere. The desert encroaches daily.

Somehow I understand the young girl's name is Hilda or Hulda. She is insistent, directive, but not mean with me. I am older than her grandmother by a few years, I judge. I am OK with it all.

As I work, I think about Estelle. How do I remember her name after all the years? She was very dark with shiny long limbs like Hulda. I don't remember ever having had a conversation with Estelle. I might have been shy or afraid or maybe she was. I was a little kid in the Bronx; Estelle would come and clean our apartment. She would hang our clothes to dry on this weird wooden contraption that my mother had. There was a stand with holes in it and wooden sticks that fit in the holes and stuck straight out into the air so you could hang small pieces of laundry. I wonder where she did the laundry. My mother used to call it the wash. In Senegal, earlier that day, I had seen the women of the village doing their wash. They had been crouching in a row, each in front of a plastic tub. Others had been carrying water in buckets, from the well, on their heads, as they chatted and laughed.

After Estelle had stopped coming to clean our house, a man named John came. He was with us for many years, until I grew up. He even came to clean my apartment when I was first married. He was dark, too, and quiet. My mother really trusted him. I don't know what ever happened to Estelle.

In Senegal, Hulda keeps me going. I sweep every room—and the dirt and the sand, bits of paper and plastic, small stones—all goes out onto the porch. In the biggest room there is some furniture. I clean it with a special cloth. Hulda makes the beds with clean sheets and picks things up from the floor. Then she leads me out into the courtyard, where women are sitting in a circle, dividing up the food from the market. There are bits of fish and some root vegetables. A very young boy is sucking a mango.

Hulda leads me to a room off the courtyard. A woman is lying on the bed and moaning softly. She is heavy and looks much older than most of the women outside. She points to her belly. She seems to be in pain. I don't know what to do although I am thinking that perhaps she is dying; I still have no idea what I am supposed to do. The woman on the bed points to an end table and Hulda reaches over for a silver card with white pills sealed in plastic pockets. She gives the pills to the woman who gestures at me with them. I shrug. I reach a hand out to the woman in blessing, an offering of my hope that she will heal.

Hulda and I leave and resume cleaning the first house. It is dark inside even though the sun is bright. There is no electricity although there is a generator and a TV. I adjust a cloth that covers the TV and Hulda readjusts it. She seems to trust my sweeping more now, however. I feel happy about that. Somehow it is important to me to please her.

I am sweating. My bruised knee is hurting (I'd fallen on it two weeks before leaving for this trip and have been limping around). I can't get down on both knees—only the left one. I am trying to pay attention to my posture as I stretch down with a flat back to mop the floor after it is swept. I use a wet rag to mop with my hands. The water in the bucket gets dirty very fast. Finally it is time to sweep the porch and mop it, too. The entire house is restored to temporary order.

Hulda motions outside to a plastic chair and bids me to sit down. She is speaking Wolof, but I understand the gesture, and I sit. Before long the older woman who was in bed calls me from her porch. She is up and about now and seems more energized. She wants me to clean her room. I get up and go over. She has her own broom, pail, and rag. I skirt the various bowls and piles that crowd the corners of her room. She observes me from the porch while I clean. I am reminded of Estelle again; I also think about all the black women who have cleaned all the kitchens and bathrooms and bedrooms of all the white women and men. I think about what hard work this is. I can't begin to imagine what this woman is thinking. There is no mathematics for this. Life has brought me here to feel this now, so I feel it—the sweat soaking my back, my burning knee, the fear that it won't be clean enough.

I am reminded that we are here to learn with our bodies and our minds so that we can enter into a new level of relationship with the world. We are here to see inequity, exploitation, deprivation, joy, harmony, courage, and love. We are here to get confused enough to continue to study and care about the global south, about Africa, about human rights, and about our responsibility as the "haves" on this globe.

Later in the week, we visit Goree Island and tour the slave house with Cherif. He is a Senegalese tour guide who speaks great English. He has a very soft, kind face. He tells us about slavery—how twenty million of the strongest and most able Africans were stolen by the traders. His voice is steely. Of those, six million died. A familiar number for the Jews. The slave house served as a storage pen for the slaves, who were treated worse than animals, viewed as non-human, property, and expendable. The first floor had the holding pens, punishment cells, and the weighing room. The slave cargo was sorted, stamped, and numbered, weighed and priced; the slave traders lived upstairs. I couldn't help thinking that we, in our privilege and wealth, live upstairs now without proper regard to what goes on beneath us.

Goree reminded me of the first time I visited Auschwitz in 1994. As we left the slave house I thanked Cherif. His eyes filled with tears and so did mine. He told us that Nelson Mandela had visited this spot in 1992 and had cried. He told us that Pope John Paul II had visited as well and apologized.

I feel overwhelmed by everything about this trip: Hilda/ Hulda, Estelle, Cherif, the glory and desecration of the Divine image. I want to say *kaddish*, as I had in Auschwitz. Those are the words that hold all the meaning that can never be spoken. We gather together: Jews who care and want to make a difference. We stand together and all together we say, *Yitgadal v'yitkadash shmey rabah:* May the great name—the name we cannot say but the name that intertwines us with all who have ever breathed or will breathe—may that unspoken Name, that great name, grow larger. May that Name—spoken and unspoken in every language on earth—grow truly sacred.

Then noisy crowds of school children arrive at the slave house for a visit. (This is a major site in all of Africa where people come to remember the slave trade.) The children are boisterous and filled with life. We go on our way.

FEELING LOST

I am feeling lost.
What do I mean by that you ask.
Something is missing.
Lost is cousin to loss.
Loss.
What could it be?
What did I lose?
Certainty. Knowing. Control. Approval.
Letting go, I fall through the atmosphere.
No longer holding on or even gripping the railings.
What a sweet blessing to be free.
And then liberation turns a corner and becomes loss, and down
    the page from loss is fear and then despair.
But, You are here with me.
Silent witness to all comings and goings, moments, and moods.
If the room is big enough, the sign says: Lost and Found
Right here.

MAR ELIAS

In 2014, our group of ten liberal North American rabbis who had traveled to Tantur had lunch at Mar Elias Monastery between Jerusalem and Bethlehem. Mar Elias means Holy Elijah. The beautiful stone structure had been built and rebuilt several times: The last time was in the twelfth century when it was rebuilt over the ruins of a Byzantine church. For eighteen centuries it has served as a way station for pilgrims traveling between Jerusalem and Bethlehem. According to the Greek Orthodox Church, it is where Elijah gave his spirit and power to John the Baptist, the forerunner of Jesus.

The Greek Orthodox bishop of Bethlehem, whose name was also Elias, was buried here in 1345. Today, the monks who live at Mar Elias cultivate grapes and olives, as they have been doing since its founding. The monastery sits on a hilltop in south Jerusalem, from which it is possible to see views of Jerusalem to the north, Bethlehem to the south, the Jerusalem neighborhood of Har Homa and the Judean desert to the east and Herodion to the southeast.

During lunch, our guide, Mohammad, shared the story of his family's displacement by the Israelis. He was not eating because it was Ramadan. He called himself a second-generation refugee. He told us that in his lifetime he had seen Jerusalem grow from six to seventy square kilometers. He had one daughter in Canada and one in Kuwait. He didn't believe that Israel wanted peace or a two-state solution. Since Yitzhak Rabin had been killed, he felt that there had been no hope. "They want to get rid of the Palestinians," he told us as we enjoyed the hummus, salad, potatoes, and fish in the spacious hall. We sat around Muhammad at the vast mahogany table, straining to hear him. We were the only visitors that day during the invasion of Gaza—Operation Protective Edge.

In the middle of the cavernous dining room there was a long glass case filled with souvenirs. Glancing in that direction, I suddenly remembered that I was supposed to be shopping for mementos from Bethlehem. I thought about how, two weeks earlier, my husband, Maynard, and our guide and translator, Regina, sat in the office of the mayor of Deveniskes, Lithuania. Maynard's mother had been born in Deveniskes in 1899 and had left with her mother, sisters, and brother in 1909. Maynard had wanted to make this trip for a long time. The mayor's office was filled with flags, souvenirs, and images of Jesus and Mary and the Holy family; it was on the town square adjacent to the cathedral, the same cathedral that Maynard's mother had walked past as a child over a century ago. The mayor was warm, animated, and gracious to us, her "returning Jews." We knew we were in a town that once had a Jewish majority. She assured us she was minding the desecrated Jewish cemetery and hoped to restore it to good condition. We didn't mention that there were no new Jews to bury there now. The mayor gave us a gift of a bottle of wine. We did not have a gift to return to her, but we accepted hers with appreciation and great shows of politeness all around.

Later that day we stopped at the home of the mayor's assistant. She also greeted us warmly, served tea, cookies, and homemade cheese. Before we left, she cut a big brick of the same cheese and pressed us to take it with us. We had no gift to return. Hence, our guide Regina suggested that, when I went to Bethlehem, I could pick up some Christian icons to send to the mayor and her assistant. She clearly wrote down their names and addresses for me.

Now, at Mar Elias, I hastened over to the large glass display case, leaving Muhammad in mid-narrative. Right away, I saw the perfect gift: a little box with a silvery crucifix in the center surrounded by four small bottles. In one bottle was holy water. In one, earth from the holy land. In another was anointing oil, and, in the fourth bottle, holy frankincense.

Holy, holy holy.

This is all so holy; so absurd and to me, so confusing. Elijah—whose name in Hebrew means *Yah is my God.* The defender of the faith. The pursuer and the pursued. The survivor who never dies. The harbinger of the Messiah who has come, who will come, who may never come.

The young man said that each little box costs two dollars. I thought that was reasonable for so much holiness. He didn't take credit cards. Only cash. I only had three one-dollar bills in my purse. He took the three dollars and gave me two little boxes—one for the mayor and one for her assistant.

I am reminded of these words by Thomas Merton, "Everything is suffering and everything is compassion."

HERRING AND HAVDALAH

It is hard to think about our trip to Lithuania without remembering the food. The best borscht I ever tasted with sour cream and boiled potatoes. I remember Regina stopping by the side of the road to pick sorrel, a green herb, and asking me, "Did you ever eat schav?" I remember the bitter schav from the Bronx. My mother would give it to my father as a huge treat: She poured it from the glass container and added sour cream. I thought it was ghastly then. But the memory is as potent as the latkes that are served everywhere with sour cream. The huge fried potato pancakes. My father loved latkes. My father was not a *Litvak*, a Jew from Lithuania. In fact, my mother degraded him as a Galician—a Galitzyaner—but he still liked the Litvak food of my mother's heritage. And there were golden blintzes, too, served, yes, with sour cream. Just like my father loved. So different from my protein and veggie diet. Not zero percent Greek yogurt, but rich, delicious sour cream! And amidst the borscht and the herring in Vilna (Vilnius, as it is now known) was the pork. Pork for breakfast, lunch, and supper. Pork in every shape and color. This we did not see at home. So strange to belong so easily to a place where you never were and are remembered by so few and forgotten by so many. Strange to see so many blonde people. Tall blonde people.

Regina is known to most Jews who pilgrimage back in time to Vilna to visit the graves of their ancestors. She is the daughter of a Soviet Jewish father and a Lithuanian mom. She introduced herself to us by saying, "I am a *shiksa*." Her father died when she was seventeen, and she embarked upon her life passion to know the Jews, their history, their teaching, their present, their languages. She knows the shtetels empty of Jews. She knows how to read the gravestones. She knows all the Jews in Vilna, including Fanya who is the librarian at the Center for Yiddish at the University and who fought with the partisans! She knows the Belarusian Jew who volunteers at the museum in Ponar where 70,000 Jews were shot and their bodies dumped into huge pits to store fuel that had been dug by the Soviets. There were photographs in that small museum of the eighty Jewish prisoners sent by the Nazis in 1943 to dig up the bodies in the pits and burn them to disguise the evidence. Regina took us to see the huge pits of ashes.

She also took us with a car and a driver near the Belarus border to Deveniskes, Devenishuk, where Maynard's mother was born. We searched for evidence of their home, the shul, the grave of his uncle who died at age three before his mother and her family left. It was an endless day. The sky turned grey and the air filled with moisture. When we returned to our hotel, there was more news of the war in Gaza. We said goodbye to Regina with great appreciation. We were on our own for Shabbat, to rest, to go the Choral synagogue for services, to collect our minds and souls.

Late Saturday afternoon we got a message from Regina that she would pick us up at 7:00 p.m. for dinner. This was not an arrangement we had made or expected, but we were ready, dressed, and curious.

She arrived with a Jewish woman from New Jersey who had just arrived from Israel: She thought we would enjoy meeting each other. She didn't have a car so we started walking. We walked beyond the tourist downtown to a residential area that did not look as well-kept: stone buildings; more litter in the streets; dogs and cats roaming. We walked for close to an hour.

It was getting cool and dark. Then we reached Regina's sister's apartment. It was spacious and crammed with old furniture, piles of papers, pottery bowls, dishes, books. Regina played the piano for us. We noshed on cheese and bread. Her nineteen-year-old son was there, and he and Maynard talked basketball: another religion. Regina served wine and herring and said, "You might not like the herring." I tasted it; it was so intense, I felt as if I had been engulfed in a salt mountain. It was not at all like the Vita Herring in cream sauce from the jar.

Then Regina asked if I would recite *havdalah!* She had a Kiddush cup. It excited her that I was a woman rabbi. We improvised the candle and the spices; I said the prayers. And I wondered: What was the *havdalah*, the separation? Between Sabbath and the week? Between before the Holocaust and after the Holocaust? Between Jews and Gentiles, herring and pork, Vilna and Vilnius? Or do we bless the heart as it breaks again and again? Or maybe it signified the temporary and unexpected separation between Maynard and me as we prepared to leave Vilna. He would be headed back home to Philadelphia, and I was to fly to Jerusalem.

Yet, the main symbol of Havdalah, the ritual of separation, is the braided candle. We have the experience of being separate, being strangers to each other and ourselves. But in the sacred time in which we share a meal, a kindness, or a prayer, and when we just sit and let be, in the breath, in the body, the mind reveals another truth. We are as connected as the strands of the havdalah candle. One color wax melts on and into the other. And as our wicks join together, there is but one bright light that streams forth.

CROSSING THE KALI GANDAKI

*My friend Rachel Cowan and I decided to join a trip sponsored by the
Karuna Center and led by our friend Paula Green. The trip was designed
to introduce supporters to the amazing work of conflict transformation that
Karuna facilitated in Nepal, one of many locations for its work. We added
on a nine-day Himalaya trek led by guides from an all-women company
called The Three Sisters. This story took place in the middle of the trek.*

We had a choice today about which path to take—the way of the
villages, the old path, or the way of the roadway—very pale fine
gray dust, lots of rocks, an occasional motorbike or bus or taxi. I
felt very aware that everything is changing. Remote Himalayan
villages are gaining access to the world of stuff.

Then we had another choice—to walk the roadway or cross
the river. This part of the great Gandaki River was mostly dry.
When the water flows, the river is black in color, due to large
amounts of glacial silt. The river forms the Kali Gandaki Gorge,
the deepest in the world—600 meters deep; it begins in the far
reaches of Upper Mustang, the forbidden kingdom, on the border
with Tibet. The gorge is named for the goddess Kali, the wild
one, fierce, fearless, and sensuous. We said we would walk in the
river.

Gita, our guide, said we would have to take off our shoes at
some point when we hit a small stream of water.

We started walking on the muddy, rock-strewn riverbed. I
said to Rachel, "It feels like we are walking in the Red Sea after it
split and the Israelites marched through on dry land."

After a while we came to a place where a group of people was milling around.

"Can you cross or do you want one of the boys to carry you?" Gita asked me.

"I can cross," I said and started to take off my two pairs of socks and my hiking boots and to attach the laces to my pack.

One of the boys who was a porter for the Spanish group (actually a group of friends trekking the same route who were all from Gerona, Catalonia) stepped up to assist me. He was very young: maybe eighteen or nineteen, with a beautiful dark brown face, gleaming eyes, straight white teeth, and a head of shiny black hair. He was shy. But suddenly he gripped my arm and took my second walking stick in his free hand. We walked into the river. I did not know his name. The river rushed by in its glacial icy blueness; it rushed very fast. The boy's grip was solid, strong, and respectful. The water was frigid cold. The rocks on the bottom hurt my pedicured feet.

I had just had my feet pedicured before leaving the United States, a practice I'd adopted in my sixties. I have a favorite place in town where the beautiful Vietnamese young woman whose English I barely understand knows me and is gentle and skilled at making these old feet look beautiful and feel soft. But at the Gandaki, I regretted how soft my feet were: The rocks really hurt.

We made it across. Rachel seemed okay. She had the help of one of the girl guides, but I noticed she was not putting her shoes back on. She was walking on the rocks. I began to understand that this was only the first of many icy crossings. There was no time to put shoes on and off; I needed to move forward through the pain. I realized that you can't see the crossings until you get there. I did not want to go forward, but I could not go back.

At that point, the young man who helped me across noticed my despair. He took off his flip-flops and offered them to me. I was astounded and overjoyed by this act of caring, by his kindness, by my gratitude, by the huge gulf of privilege, culture, language, and age that had been crossed because of his attentiveness and goodwill.

I nodded and smiled at him and put the flip-flops on my feet. He took my arm.

We continued walking through the riverbed. We forged the next icy stream and then the one after that.

I was so happy.

I thought my young friend was happy, too.

I said, *"Danyavad"*—thanks in Nepali. I said, *"Namaste."* *Namaste* is the ordinary greeting in Nepal—it means "The Divine in me sees the Divine in you."

An act of kindness dispels the illusion of separateness and reaffirms that no one is a stranger.

PART IV

LOVE AND
GRATITUDE

As I mentioned in the Introduction to this book, in our everyday lives, the stranger is sometimes the refugee, sometimes the person of color, age, youth, accent, small or large body, deafness, blindness, baldness, or different view, different neighborhood, different family or lover, profession, or power. There is no limit to who can be the stranger. In fact, some of our most challenging strangers may be those we live with and those we have loved or tried to love.

Mordecai Kaplan writes: "The salvation that the modern man or woman seeks in this world . . . has a personal and social significance . . . Selfish salvation is impossibility. . . There can be no personal salvation so long as injustice and strife exist in the social order; there can be no social salvation so long as the greed for gain and the lust for domination are permitted to inhibit the hunger for human fellowship and sympathy in the hearts of men and women" *(The Meaning of God in Modern Jewish Religion,* 53–54).

This is all connected to the radical work of love. This love is not of our making, but it exists. It is the antidote to anger and cynicism. It realizes the profound interconnection of all life. Love widens our perspective, enlarges and creates space for creativity and surprise. It doesn't contract in fear. It doesn't polarize. It sees the universal potential both to hide and to hurt. It knows that change is possible. The love I am talking about is not a feeling or a whim. It is not puppy love. It is an evolving outgrowth of intention, practice, letting go again and again, studying and praying, and living within a beloved community. Love is immovable, impartial goodwill.

A MOMENT AGO

A moment ago a tear came down my cheek.
I was afraid you didn't love me.
Then I remembered,
of course you do.
My fear makes me forget.
My tear let me remember.

TZELEM ELOHIM—
MY SHADOW PASSES THROUGH GOD'S HEART

In breath out breath
Tzelem elohim
Forgive me
Tzelem elohim
You are forgiven
Tzlem elohim
Rebellion—*tzelem elohim*
Return—*tzelem elohim*
Surrounded by every one who has ever loved me
Receiving that love in every bone, muscle, cell
Tzelem elohim

Tzel—Shadow
Mem—Middle letter
Shadow in the middle, in the mikvah, mayim
Shadow of God dipping in the waters

Tzelem elohim

My shadow passing through God's heart

Tzelem Elohim
Let me look into your eyes

Tzelem elohim
Ten fingers
Ten toes

How could I harm this one?
Tzelem elohim

In the subway—*tzelem elohim*
Old age—*tzelem elohim*
Tahara—wash the dead
The human is a Divine Image
Clothe the naked, free the bound, heal the sick

Imagine you are surrounded by all the people in the world who
    have ever loved you
Tzelem elohim
And you are capable of receiving that love
Tzelem elohim

Red, orange, yellow, green, blue, indigo, violet
Tzelem elohim

How could I ever hurt you?
Tzelem elohim
How could I ever hate you?
Tzelem elohim

YOM KIPPUR AT LINCOLN MEMORIAL SEPTEMBER 2015

Today is a day of repentance, renewal, and solidarity.
Repentance in Hebrew is *T'shuvah,* which means turning and
   returning—making an about-face.
It is a most treasured human gift.
One who turns around and heads in the right direction
   Is respected and appreciated.
Indeed, when we say that we are lost, it is often the beginning of
   the journey home.
The Source of Life, the Divine Beloved, calls us to return, calls us
   to *T'shuvah,* again and again.

V'Shavta Ad Adonai Elohecha: "And you shall return to Godliness,
   to Goodness" it says in the Book of Deuteronomy.

"Return," the tradition says, "the moment before you die."
"But when will I die?" we ask.
"No one knows. So return today!"

Return from where?

Return from arrogance, fear and delusion,
Return from a false view that to say we are wrong means we are
   weak and foolish instead of strong and wise and loving,
From a false hope that our children and their children will not
   harvest the consequences of our greed.

Turn toward what?

Turn us toward remembering

Turn us toward remembering what we learn in the Book of Leviticus—when God tells us, *Ki Lee Haaretz, ki Gerim V'Toshavim Atem Emadi*—The land is mine—you are sojourners and resident settlers with me. Our ownership and our residency are conditional and impermanent.

Turn us toward remembering that all beings on this planet, all beings, breathe the same air, are burned by the same sun, eat from the same soil and drink from the same cup.

Turn us toward remembering that all beings on this planet, all beings, are loved by the same endless, everlasting and infinite Love.

Turn us toward remembering that there is only one body to wound, and it is ours.
Hasheveinu Adonai Elecha V'Nashuva
Chadesh Yamaynu Kekedem
Turn us to you, Adonai, and we will return.
Renew every single one of our days.

May the ancient wisdom guide us into a new world of caring and hope.

YOUR WILL

For the millionth time.
In the grove of sitka spruce
on Grief island Alaska
everything became clear.

I am in this world for one reason alone, to learn to love.
"What am I meant to do?" I ask as I grasp the dappled brown
    red bark.
The answer arises.
"Be an instrument of this creation. Take every inch of wound,
    criticism, judgment, lack, loss, and cast it into the golden sea.
"Cast it into the sea the way the sailors cast Jonah during the
    storm, when he thought he was going to Tarshish but ended
    up going to Nineveh in the end."

YOM KIPPUR

Who is beseeching Heaven?
Who is crying out *"Avinu Malkaynu?"*
Who is confessing their emptiness?
Whose deeds just don't measure up?
Who is logging their great list of needs?
To be heard, to be filled, to be held, forgiven, remembered,
    answered, healed, protected.
Who?

You and me.
Jews in high-ceilinged temples and basement shuls,
settlers in Ariel and Hebron,
pregnant Jewish women,
recent converts, gay and trans Jews,
hungry Jews, Black and Brown Jews,
old, tired, and sick Jews,
teenagers and bored Jews, crying and laughing Jews,
Jewish soldiers
Jewish generals and judges,
Jews in prison,
married Jews, divorced, single, and widowed Jews,
Jews in power,
Jewish Republicans and Jewish Democrats and Jewish Greens,
Zionists, non-Zionists, anti-Zionists, post-Zionists.
in fur coats and white cotton kittels
in Nikes and leather high heels,

at the Wall,
in the hall,
at the overflow service,
everyone.

Avinu Malkaynu,
We are all empty.
You are full.
Fill us with justice.
Fill us with love.
Help us!

HEALING IN THE FAMILY

We can all tell stories of a time when we experienced liberation through the tools of mindfulness. I'll tell you one of mine
to remind you of one of yours. Together we can recall them and
honor them as fruits of this practice.

I was married for eleven years to my husband Steve, and we
had two children. In our thirty-plus divorced years, we had a lot
of drama, including fights over the kids, money, and who did
what to whom. I lived with a huge amount of anger. I repressed
some of it, acted out some of it, drank over a fair amount of it.
Our children grew up and married and we remarried as well.
We managed to get through the two weddings, even shared the
baby namings of two grandchildren. The burning animosity was
gone. The relationship was cool. OK. Our kids never mentioned
either of us to the other one. I got sober and was introduced to
mindfulness.

Years passed. A few weeks before Pesach, our son decided to
make a Seder. He invited his sister, her kids, his wife's sister and
kids, his mother-in-law, and his father. I phoned to ask him if I
could come, too. I had no real doubts that I could be perfectly
polite and enjoy being with the family. My son didn't phone
me back. My daughter wouldn't discuss it. Finally my son told
me they would rather I did not come. Well, I saw it—the huge
eruption of difficult feelings—all arise in my mind. I felt it. It
was painful. The rejection. The anger. The sense of isolation. The
personal slight. The injustice and unfairness. I was silent. Amaz-

ing. I didn't say anything except: "OK." I made my own Seder. I sat with the feelings. They were unpleasant. They moved through my chest and my throat. I didn't give a huge amount of airtime to the old stories. I talked about it a little but not as a victim. I was curious. I was waiting to see what would be revealed. It hurt, but somehow I knew I needed to wait. Sometimes I think this is the greatest gift we receive from mindfulness—waiting and listening.

After the Seder I had a conversation with my son. "What was that all about?" I asked him. "Well, Mom," he said. "We feel that we are not the ones to initiate a change in your relationship with Dad. If you want things to change you have to be the ones to initiate it." I sat with that. I was not at all sure I understood what he was saying. I waited. I prayed to understand. I felt the emptiness, the confusion, and I saw the ancient, unwholesome reactions of self-righteousness knocking at the doors of perception. Weeks passed. I counted the *Omer*.

Then, at the end of May, our third grandchild was born. I saw Steve as soon as I reached the synagogue where the *bris* was to take place. He had just finished eleven months of saying *kaddish* for his father. I went up to him and out of my mouth came words I didn't know I even had. I said I wanted to share the joy with him of our children and our grandchildren. I wanted to be connected to him and his wife in a real way, in an open and free way. A few days letter we set up a coffee date for the four of us, Steve and me and our spouses. Starbucks on Columbus Ave and West Eighty-sixth Street. We sat for two hours. We talked about our kids, the grandkids, how much we love them, how much we care. We did not review the past. The past doesn't matter. Somehow we all knew this was a new beginning.

Since then it has really been different. We have shared dinners and just regular times without a big deal. Just people. Our kids are even almost used to it. It took so long. It feels so good. There is no one there to compete or fight or be right anymore.

There was no one who *did* anything. It was more like undoing. The undoing is a consequence of the practice, of space, of God's presence—who knows? It is like Hadassah said at her sixth birthday with four grandparents, from her mother's side alone (she has four from her dad too): "It's good to be with my family." She knows. The kids know.

It is not difficult to see the value of mindfulness in dealing with unwholesome mind states such as anger. One illustration of working with anger on larger, more complex canvases, comes from comments I often hear from social activists that they need their own anger at injustice to fuel their activism. They don't want to relinquish anger: They consider inciting anger to be a method of organizing for activism on behalf of a just cause. They often ask, understandably, "What about righteous indignation? How can we *not* be consumed by wrath at the wanton destruction of the land, water, air, and species of our home in the cosmos, the living earth—God's creation? And how could we not be fuming when we contemplate the unjust distribution of earth's abundance perpetrated by so much corruption, violence, and greed?" Their questions are valid and crucial.

Perhaps Jewish tradition intimates a response. We have figures that display great anger—such as Moses, Elijah, and the Prophets—who are revered as great moral heroes. It is true, however, that, when Moshe strikes the rock seeking water, this act of anger is later recalled as the reason he was not allowed to enter the Promised land. In other words, our anger will only get us so far and not further. We are also challenged, not infrequently, by a depiction of the Israelite God beset by rage attacks and angered to the point of wanting to blot out the people he loves. (Ever feel that way?) However, the rabbis who craft the Judaism we know and practice choose to lift up the side of God that is compassion, forgiveness, and kindness. The thirteen attributes of God's eternal love form the center of the holiest day of the year, Yom Kippur, and God as the source of *chesed* and *rachamim*, mercy and compassion fill the pages of our siddur. Perhaps the rabbis are inviting us into the possibility of emulating the Divine as we transform our own anger into the empathy that fosters connection and forgiveness.

ADON OLAM

Eternal power of all time and space,
all that is hidden and revealed.
Cosmic Infinitesimal,
I rest in your hand,
I hold hands with you,
I am your hand and
I am your feet.
Walking toward you,
with you,
for you,
as a seal of peace
mothering the wounded one.

BURYING THE FORESKIN

Ezra calls one morning. Well, I really call him first. He is so on my mind, especially me being in Boulder while he is in Jerusalem. I emailed him that verse from Yehuda Halevi. *Ani B'sof maarav.* I am in the outer limits of the West. *Libi b'mizrach.* But my heart is in Jerusalem. In the East. Boulder and Jerusalem. The folks in Boulder loved Ezra when he was their student rabbi. I was introduced here as "Ezra's Mom." We enter that strange teepee-shaped sanctuary of the Renewal synagogue in Boulder. I stare at the tapestry of the *sephirot,* the Divine spheres, the shades of greys and blues and glass shimmering behind the thin cloth—the light barely perceptible.

On this particular morning Ezra tells me that he buried Benjy's foreskin at Robinson's Arch. I think of the blue sky in Jerusalem amidst the hills, and I see the cerulean sky on that luminous day in Boulder surrounded by mountains. I recall the arch of stones, remnant of one that once stood at the southwestern corner of the Temple Mount built during the reconstruction of the Second Temple at the end of the first century BCE. It was uncovered in the eighteenth century and named for the archaeologist. It is the place offered to the women instead of the Wall as a sacred but not equal prayer place. It is a place of hurt and protest—twenty-five years of wanting of the Women at the Wall, wrapped in *talesim, talitot* embroidered with purple and crimson birds and flowers. Dangling earrings, babies in pouches.

Ezra tells me he buried Benjy's foreskin at Robinson's Arch and I say, "Wow, that is amazing." As my mind goes blank, as I blink, pass to the next topic, notice call-waiting and pick it up. Then hours later I am teaching mindful parenting and grand parenting. I mention this mysterious act. A beautiful man in a knitted *kippah*, a short beard with more than hints of gray, and a very sweet smile, helps me understand. He tells me he is a hugger and his quilted nylon vest feels cool when we hug. He organized the workshop and heard me speak about Ezra's dad. We divorced and I left town when Ezra was the same age Benjy is now—two and a half. I speak about how the hatred has dissolved after decades, as we have grown gray and too tired to hate each other or even to remember much anymore. Such a blessing—two grown, married children and three grandchildren. I can look at him and feel ease between us; relaxed now, we can even laugh. There is affection and deep gratitude for what we share.

This past Sukkot, Steve and I were co-grandparents for Benjy at the retreat center where Ezra led the prayers. We shared a *lulav* and *etrog*. We stood next to each other and he passed the palm branch to me and then I passed it back to him. We shared the long pointy palm branches and the perfumed myrtle and the still green willow. We smelled the sweet, sour sacred smell of the golden citron. We blessed together—side to side—and praised God for this day, for the healing, for the beauty of our son Ezra and his son Benjy climbing endlessly up and down the slide outside.

Then Ezra went to Jerusalem and he saw the arch that connected his parents who were torn asunder when he was the age of his son. And the arch bridges the differences. The arch unites the severed halves of the heart. It makes a whole. Ezra saw that the foreskins of our hearts, all our hearts, have been circumcised. Then he buried Benjy's foreskin at Robinson's Arch.

BABIES: POEM TO BE READ AT A BABY NAMING

Dear God,
I notice babies now.
Slumping in their white plastic buckets,
wheeled along in orange plaid strollers.
I notice their plump cheeks and their big round eyes.
How they stare at me
when I smile and make funny sounds.
I notice what babies wear
and if they have teeth or hair.
I can't get enough of them.

I see You when I see them.
Like some people see You when they sit with the dying.
The veil is thinner at the edges.

I want to caress, embrace, and cherish every baby in the world.
I want to kiss their little baby hands and feet—
their pudgy fingers and their perfect toes.

Babies hold all Your promise.
Please don't let us let them down!
Keep them in our sight always to remind us of our innocence and
    Your love.

BE YOUR AWAKENED HEART

Waking up is like doing yoga.
It takes strength, flexibility, and balance
and it is a lot easier when you breathe.
We are all yogis—spiritual warriors with hearts that keep
breaking open so that the light of God's love keeps shining
through.

How do we keep our balance?
It is not easy.

But we begin.

We take a stable stance on the four corners of our feet. We root
deep into the earth.
Then we let go into the greater whole, the fullness of the eternal
breath that accompanies every leap into risk.

One of my favorite images of living this life is from the autobiography of Ginger Rogers. She was the beautiful dance partner of Fred Astaire, and he was always acclaimed as the greatest dancer and she was just his partner. Her story is called: "Dancing Backwards in High Heels." She did all the moves he did but did them backwards and in high heels. That is a lot like our lives. Moving into the future without knowing what it will bring and yet doing it with integrity, grace, and trust.

And I guess we need to remember that we do have a partner in this business.

And we can remember that when we breathe.
we are breathed.
And we *are* dancing backwards in high heels.
But we are not alone.

May we feel the strength, flexibility, and balance.
May we all meet the depth of the love in our hearts.
May we all remember, again and again, that we are not alone.

May we all remember, again and again, the possibility of blessing.
Because we know that, when we bless, we become whole.

May we remember to bless a ripe tomato and a political victory—
    even a very tiny one.
May we remember to bless the face of a friend after a long
    absence.
May we remember to bless the salty smell of the ocean, a beauti-
    ful tune, or a pure turn of phrase.
May we remember to bless a good person's life and death, the
    snow coming down and the sun coming up.

When we search our heart, we remember that the way to do
    is to be.
Be who you truly are, dear friend,
be exactly who you are,
and that is the well of blessing.

NINE DAYS WITH THE GRANDKIDS

We tell my daughter and son-in-law that for their tenth wedding anniversary we would take the kids for nine days while they celebrate by traveling to a beautiful place to enjoy a fabulous couples' retreat. The kids are not babies anymore. Hadassah is almost nine and Yehuda is five and a half. Part of the lure is five days at Ocean City, New Jersey—the shore.

We rent a suite in a hotel so that we can do most of our cooking there. We are about two blocks from the beach. I lay down some ground rules about how many treats the kids could have. There are eating treats and there are take-away treats. The boardwalk is treat heaven for kids (and not so bad for grown-ups). It's all color and fluff and glitter. One could say that being on the beach is a big enough treat. I love it. The squish of the sand, the endless roar of the waves, the smell, the skin, the lack of pretense and apology. It's the beach after all. This is a great family-oriented beach. Tons of kids and parents and grandparents. Most people are in a great mood. Who needs more treats? Still, we come to a mutually agreed upon treat treaty, and the kids are great, holding the line and not asking for more. One food treat per day, two take-homes—and one lunch out and one dinner out! Not too bad.

There are many boardwalk shops. By coincidence, some are staffed by young Lithuanians! Yehuda decides he wants his first take-home treat to be a penguin Beanie Baby. Despite Hadassah's other suggestions that he branch out, he decides that his second take-away treat would also be a Beanie Baby penguin in a different color. This was not that easy to find because the brand needs to be Beanie Baby and the species, penguin. Owls and unicorns, bears and puppies simply would not do. Yehuda ceremoniously names each penguin. The blue one is Sparkle and the gray one is Sparky. I am reminded of my nephew Josh who died suddenly of a massive heart attack in his early forties. He was a passionate defense attorney, a loving son and brother, uncle and husband. Josh loved to argue and challenge the conventional view of most anything. He was also a lifelong collector of Beanie Babies—of all colors, shapes, species, and sizes—until his untimely death. I am moved to view Yehuda's sudden collecting passion (he declares his intention to keep collecting, but in a pristine, self-determined order) as a memorial to Josh of blessed memory.

We have a great time at the beach and still have two nights at home before the parents' return. We do the laundry, and, since the kids live only a few buildings away in the same development, we put most of their clean stuff away before the parents come home. Somehow the Beanie Babies end up at nighttime in the apartment where the kids are *not* sleeping. I do have one beanie baby from Josh's collection. She is a mid-size purple bear, named Princess Diana. Hadassah claims her for a sleeping partner. Yehuda ends up without a sleep mate. He is pretty distraught.

In a moment of grace, insight, and Divine deliverance, I glance at the corner of the bedroom where the suitcases, yoga blocks, and assorted airplane neck pillows are stashed. I spy a soft, blue, very pliable silky pillow, and I say to Yehuda, "Sweetheart, you can sleep with Clumpy. He is very cuddly and sweet. He doesn't have a face or a body but still he is super huggable and lovable." Yehuda turns to me with those big brown eyes. "Okay, Grandma!!" As I am handing Clumpy over to Yehuda, Hadassah pipes up, "I'll sleep with Clumpy." "Come on, give me a break," Yehuda says. "You have Diana." Then he wraps his little arms around Clumpy and promptly falls asleep. The concealed is revealed. The source of all tender love is as close as this moment of turning toward.

My soul blesses the Mystery, the Energy, the name of the Nameless. You are very great. You fill the cosmos with light. You shine from our eyes. You inhabit everything. Your majesty and splendor are inherent in all things. Our soul sees You. The children see You. I see You. Thanks for Clumpy.

BIRTHDAY BLESSING

May I live with an open heart
like the purple iris on the mountain.
Just here.
Like the rock in the stream,
like the pine saplings not knowing if they will make it to fall.
Just like the rest of us.
We don't know either.
But it's nearly spring and the sun is shining.
May I live with an open heart.
May all that blocks my heart dissolve,
like the warm honey in the hot tea.

TRUST THE PATH

It is my birthday and I want to get to the top of the mountain so
    I can sing happy birthday to myself.
Anyway.
I am climbing and on the way I hear, "Trust the path."
I have trusted the path and I do trust the path except when I
    forget or get scared or overwhelmed.
So I keep going.
I find walking sticks.
I am out of breath.
I see the wild flowers.
Purple and bright yellow. I look up and someone is walking down
wearing an orange vest.
Is it a man or a woman?
A hunter perhaps.
Maybe I should be wearing an orange vest.
And finally we meet on the path.
And it is my dear friend who knows it is my birthday.
She gives me a huge smile and a silent hug.

AHAVAH RABBAH

What is a great love?
A love that reaches deep inside our hearts and minds and never
    departs.
An expanding, continually surpassing compassion that flows
    toward and within us.

Those who came before us were blessed to learn how it truly is.
So may we have the merit to be open to this learning.

May we know that we are held in an embrace of infinite kindness.
May we become still.
Still enough to hear,
still enough to get clear,
still enough to know suffering and its release.
May we embody this wisdom.
May it shine from our eyes
as the love that it is.

May our minds and hearts be unified to behold with love and
    wonder
that which is ever becoming.

No more victims, no more powerlessness, no more blaming or
    shaming each other and ourselves.

For our faith in this,
in this sacred this, makes us joyous.

Continually gathering peacefully from the dispersed and distracted into this right here, our home.

We engage in an ever faithful and mysterious process of drawing closer to your name, what is, sacred love.

ANA B'KOACH

This quintessential mystical prayer is chanted right before L'cha Dodi on Friday night and each night after counting the Omer between Passover and Shavuot. It does not contain any names for God but rather is considered to be a name of God composed of forty-two letters. It represents a complete offering of the self, the ego, one's attachments, to the One.

I offer myself
To the Greatness and Goodness of all that is
to untie these knots.

To participate in and yield
to this process of purification in joy.
To be blessed, released, held in mercy and forgiven right now.

To accept the tender unfolding guidance that always appears.

To once again have my sacred center mirrored in the Eternal One.

Receive our suffering!
Listen to our outcry!
You, who know all the hidden mysteries.

KI ANU AMECHA: BECAUSE WE ARE YOUR PEOPLE

Ki Anu Amecha *is an early medieval poem, which expands the well-known verse in the Song of Songs, "I am my Beloved's and my Beloved is mine."* Ani L'Dodi V'Dodi Li.

It is about closeness, relationship, dependence; inviting a sense of care to our own worried minds.

It is a way to remember that things do not always have to be the same. More love, hope, energy can be ignited.

A circle of empathy is cast across the great divide between the finite and the infinite, between human and Divine, between the limited imperfect and that which knows and contains all.

I like to translate the word *"Ki"* in *Ki anu amecha* as "because."

Because we are Your people, You are our Ruler.

This is an affirmation of mutuality. We turn toward the Infinite. We acknowledge a relationship. That acknowledgment creates its own reality.

We show up and say: Here we are with all our flaws, the way you created us. Yet, we also know that we partake of something wondrous and brilliant. We call you toward us. Because we are your children, you are our parent. Because we are Your beloved, You are our friend. We turn toward You and your power is revealed in our very being.

What is it like to be in relationship with the Infinite? What is it like to be a friend of the Creator's? What is it like to be a sheep in the flock of the Holy One of Blessing? Can we allow ourselves to feel that amount of care, blessing, support, guidance?

Do we think we are worthy to be in this relationship?

The answer of our tradition is a resounding "YES!"
We are worthy and deserving of infinite love and care. Each and
every one of us!!!
One beautiful verse reads—*Ki anu segulatecha v'ata krovaynu.* We
are Your cherished ones and You are near to us. Because we
are Your cherished ones, You are near to us.

Take this moment
breathe into our inner body.
Breath is a trustworthy manifestation of God's continuing care
for us.

As you allow your awareness to expand and grow, you might feel
the buoyancy of the breath inside your body; you might feel a
sense of lightness, sweetness, a sense of being cherished and
beloved.
Allow this to expand.

If you are able, turn to someone close to you and say to each
other: "You are a precious child of the beloved."
Feel that truth echo in your body.
I will sit with you both as you feel that truth.

Let us take a moment to rest in being cherished and close, worthy, and beloved.

Let us celebrate the source of all that is possible.

Each of us is a precious child of the beloved.
We know we all have our imperfections.
But now let us take this moment to rest in being cherished and
close, worthy, and beloved.
Let's celebrate the source of all that is possible.

THE GIFTS

Dear Lisa came up with four ways to say goodbye to me when I left the staff of the Institute (IJS). Four gifts. Quite amazing! The first was the dinner with the staff. I remember driving to Westchester, which always makes me anxious because I remember being nauseous as a kid in the back of my father's Oldsmobile on Sundays as we drove to visit my sister and brought bagels and lox. I dislike Westchester County. People drive too fast in too many lanes of traffic. I am always confused. I get lost, and then I sink inside into the little dark-eyed girl—lonely, sad, and lost.

I went just for dinner because it didn't make sense for me to be part of the "staff retreat" if I was no longer on the "staff." The evening wasn't fun for me; I was annoyed that I had to drive seven hours round trip to have a meal I was not so happy about. The food was pasta. I don't like pasta. That's all I remember.

The second gift was a dinner at Rachel's. It was in New York City. Maynard drove with me and we miraculously found a perfect parking spot. I love her light-filled, pink and mauve apartment overlooking the Hudson River. I love Rachel. Abby and Nathan were there. The food was perfect. There was nothing with onions and garlic, which make me sick. I was very happy. After dinner, people sat around in the living room and spoke about me. It was weird. I could not take it in. I felt hot and cold at the same time. The words floated overhead like those balloons in the cartoons. My heart, my mind, and my skin were tight. The words weren't landing. I couldn't understand whom they were talking about. But they are all such lovely people; I was sure they were sincere.

The third gift was the interview at the IJS retreat in California with Marc. That was fun. My hair looked good and I was wearing the right clothes. The Institute spent serious money to hire a professional LA film crew. The lighting was spectacular. So was the sound. Marc prepared perfect questions, caring and thoughtful. I was both relaxed and lit up—both from within and without. Marc made me feel comfortable with his smooth voice, his warm features, his dark curly hair, and the sweet, concerned way he smiled and lifted his eyebrows.

The fourth and last gift was "the book." I have now received it. It is beautiful. One hundred people wrote, saying in their own words and style how much they have learned from me. Truly I have been a teacher of wisdom and love to them. It seems impossible to grasp and believe. How can I embrace this love in humility? This is the essence of mature humility.

Dear God, Please help me take in the blessings and the gratitude while I shed the ego, the embarrassment, and fear that wrap and birth the ego. Let me know that I do belong here. Right here on this sacred journey. I have been given the gift to know my purpose. To console Ida, my mother, I was born. To console others and teach consolation and liberation, I have lived my life. Thank you.

SIMU LEV—PLACE YOUR HEART—MEDIEVAL PIYYUT

This medieval liturgical poem offers sage advice. We are instructed to pay attention to our soul. It is our treasure.

Pay attention to the soul
Opal, amethyst and gold.
Its light is like the sun's
More radiant than seventy morning stars.
Kissed by the moon of Adar bet,
Greeted by Venus herself.
Light.
Cosmic light
Calling us home.
Rising from the ankle bones through the spine,
Joining, looping,
Roots to crown,
Restoring her to her glory
Which never fades.
Nowhere to go but here.

HALLOWEEN IN NEW YORK CITY

It is Halloween. I am picking up my five-and-a-half-year-old grandson, Benjy, at his Orthodox Jewish day school. He is in kindergarten. The school is in Riverdale at 254th Street. I take the Metro North train from Grand Central Station, which hugs the mighty Hudson River, and trudge up the hill to the school. Benjy is all ready when I arrive.

There is no sign that it is Halloween. All Saints Day, even in its secular garb, has a distinctly Christian scent. Neither Benjy nor I mention that it is Halloween. We start walking up the longer steep hill. As usual, he stops to pick up sticks, branches, random acorns, pinecones. He likes to whack the sticks against the bushes. He looks for patches of mud and puddles to step into. I look for his little hand to hold in the face of the ongoing traffic heading down the hill we are climbing up.

At the top we wait for the bus on Riverdale Avenue. It will take us through the Bronx, across to Manhattan and eventually to Washington Heights where he lives. It finally arrives and we climb on board. Luckily, there are lots of empty seats today. We get two seats together and Benjy takes the one by the window. Once we pass into Manhattan, it begins. Children of all sizes and shapes, and grown-ups, too, are in costume, parading up and down Broadway, trick-or-treating at retail stores—bakeries, bodegas, hairdressers, drugstores, auto tag places. All the shop-keepers seem to have an endless supply of candy to deliver to the paraders.

Benjy is looking out the window. He is exuberant. "There is

Captain America!" he shrieks. "There is Batman! There's Elsa!" he squeals. "There's Wonder Woman!!!" He is pointing in delight, identifying one character after another, one Halloweener after another emerging from fantasy to life.

Does he realize what is happening? Does he understand that it is Halloween? Does he know what that means? Or, does he believe this is just what is happening—a parade of characters that are in the books and posters in his bedroom but are as real to him as his teachers or his grandma? I don't know.

Finally we arrive at our stop on 181st Street where the parade of trick-or-treaters is robust. We see grown-ups in costume and even a dog dressed up. It all seems totally natural to Benjy. He still doesn't mention Halloween, wanting a costume or even the candy giveaway. He is just filled with delight. There is a surprising absence of craving or comparing.

He does want his treat from Grandma at Dunkin' Donuts. Lately he wants me to buy him a Boston Kreme Donut. We enter Dunkin' Donuts but before I have a chance to order, the man behind the counter hands Benjy a pumpkin munchkin. Free. Apparently, this is the standard Dunkin' treat for the trick or treaters. Benjy happily accepts the munchkin and pops it in his mouth. No comment. Nothing unusual. Then I buy the Boston Kreme. We sit down as he very mindfully, with enormous focus, consumes the donut.

We leave Dunkin' Donuts and at the next corner a man is sitting in front of the diner handing out candy from a large box on his lap. As we pass by, the man offers Benjy a Tootsie Pop. Benjy happily accepts it, swiftly opens it and pops it in his mouth. I prompt, "Say thank you." He does. At first he thinks there is bubble gum in the center but soon the tootsie-roll center is revealed. He is very pleased. No big deal, though. This generosity on this day is simply what is happening. He can enjoy it, accept it. It is the flow of life, the arising and passing of all that is, ever new, ever curious, ever alive. I marvel at the innocence, the open-ness, and the freedom.

This little boy seems to possess the art of living in two civilizations. He enjoys what is not truly his to celebrate, and he embraces it with wonder and pleasure as it touches him. Maybe this is a model of living with difference—the possibility of true pluralism. Maybe it is also a vision of equanimous mind. As the Halloweeners of desire, aversion, delusion, and confusion arise and pass, can we remain at rest in the spacious sky of this eternal fleeting moment?

PART V

**INTERPRETATIONS
OF PSALMS,
GUIDED PRACTICES,
AND REFLECTIONS
ON TEACHING**

The Book of Psalms in the Hebrew Bible is a compilation of 150 religious poems. They have been translated into every known language,
prayed by devout Jews and Christians for millennia, and studied by
scholars of language and history. The Psalms have been set to music,
carved into marble, chanted, danced, and used in meditation. The
psalms that follow are free-flowing translations that were inspired by
sitting in silent meditation. I contemplated the words and the meaning and then offered a rendition that spoke clearly to my own experience. They reflect a willingness to work with the mind and to see
that effort as Divine service. The hope is to transform the sometimes
archaic and stiff language into a language of the heart, a language of
liberation and clear seeing.

The psalms are followed by a variety of guided practices inspired
by themes of the Torah. They offer some concrete ways to release
one's limited ideas and impressions as we learn to embrace both
the stranger within and the stranger before us. They might be aids
in your practice or tools in your teaching. Many of the pieces include
questions. We ask ourselves questions to inspire curiosity and interest. These factors free us from fixed views and entrenched ideas of
what is true. These questions can lead us toward mystery where we
discover the deeper truths of existence.

PSALM 27

לְדָוִד: יְהוָה, אוֹרִי וְיִשְׁעִי—
מִמִּי אִירָא; יְהוָה מָעוֹז־חַיַּי,
מִמִּי אֶפְחָד.

Awareness is sunlight in the
mind. No one can take that
from me. Awareness is my life's
stronghold. It absorbs all fear.

בִּקְרֹב עָלַי, מְרֵעִים–לֶאֱכֹל
אֶת־בְּשָׂרִי צָרַי וְאֹיְבַי לִי; הֵמָּה
כָשְׁלוּ וְנָפָלוּ.

The hindrances and defilements
are as close as my flesh and
mind, but they dissolve in the
light of being known.

אִם־תַּחֲנֶה עָלַי, מַחֲנֶה–לֹא־
יִירָא לִבִּי: אִם־תָּקוּם עָלַי,
מִלְחָמָה–בְּזֹאת, אֲנִי בוֹטֵחַ.

Even though I feel assaulted
by hostile forces, my heart
remains confident, balanced
and patient.

אַחַת, שָׁאַלְתִּי מֵאֵת־יְהוָה–
אוֹתָהּ אֲבַקֵּשׁ: שִׁבְתִּי בְּבֵית־
יְהוָה, כָּל־יְמֵי חַיַּי; לַחֲזוֹת
בְּנֹעַם־יְהוָה, וּלְבַקֵּר בְּהֵיכָלוֹ.

I seek only one thing, one
thing alone: to connect to this
moment. Nowhere else. Only
this. Nothing less. My palace
in time.

כִּי יִצְפְּנֵנִי, בְּסֻכֹּה–בְּיוֹם רָעָה:
יַסְתִּרֵנִי, בְּסֵתֶר אָהֳלוֹ; בְּצוּר,
יְרוֹמְמֵנִי.

When difficulties arise, I have a
hiding place in my own heart—
a secret tent where I can go
and feel safe, a rock to rest my
head upon.

וְעַתָּה יָרוּם רֹאשִׁי, עַל אֹיְבַי
סְבִיבוֹתַי, וְאֶזְבְּחָה בְאָהֳלוֹ,
זִבְחֵי תְרוּעָה; אָשִׁירָה
וַאֲזַמְּרָה, לַיהוָה.

Greed, hatred, and delusion
don't stop coming, but when
they are met with a spacious
heart, they don't stick around.
Leaving me so grateful, I want to
sing out loud:

שְׁמַע־יְהוָה קוֹלִי אֶקְרָא;
וְחָנֵּנִי וַעֲנֵנִי.

Listen, world! The power of love
sets me free.

לְךָ, אָמַר לִבִּי–בַּקְּשׁוּ פָנָי;
אֶת־פָּנֶיךָ יְהוָה אֲבַקֵּשׁ.

When I turn to face my heart—
then everyone and everything is
revealed.

אַל־תַּסְתֵּר פָּנֶיךָ, מִמֶּנִּי–אַל
תַּט־בְּאַף, עַבְדֶּךָ: עֶזְרָתִי הָיִיתָ;
אַל־תִּטְּשֵׁנִי וְאַל־תַּעַזְבֵנִי,
אֱלֹהֵי יִשְׁעִי.

Let this truth not be hidden from
me. If only I could remember
always what seems so clear right
now. Wisdom would guide my
every moment.

כִּי־אָבִי וְאִמִּי עֲזָבוּנִי; וַיהוָה
יַאַסְפֵנִי.

Awareness and compassion
would be a father and a mother
to me.

הוֹרֵנִי יְהוָה, דַּרְכֶּךָ: וּנְחֵנִי,
בְּאֹרַח מִישׁוֹר–לְמַעַן, שׁוֹרְרָי.

But I can follow the guidance of
those who have walked this path
before.

אַל־תִּתְּנֵנִי, בְּנֶפֶשׁ צָרָי: כִּי
קָמוּ־בִי עֵדֵי־שֶׁקֶר, וִיפֵחַ חָמָס.

Trying to stay alert to the
obstacles along the way because
delusion and hatred aren't disappearing so fast.

לוּלֵא–הֶאֱמַנְתִּי, לִרְאוֹת
בְּטוּב־יְהוָה: בְּאֶרֶץ חַיִּים.

Still, I affirm my faith in the
power of goodness.

קַוֵּה, אֶל־יְהוָה: חֲזַק,
וְיַאֲמֵץ לִבֶּךָ; וְקַוֵּה, אֶל־יְהוָה.

May we take courage; may we
be strong; may our hearts be
so filled with love there is no
room for anything else! May
we see the arising and passing
of all conditioned things. May
we open to the Unconditioned:
Y*H*V*H

WHAT ARE YOU ASKING FOR?
ACHAT SHALTI MEI-EIT ADONAI OTAH AVAKEISH

One thing I ask of Adonai, only that do I seek.
Imagine if you could ask one thing of Adonai.

Imagine if reality, life, all the power and resources in existence
could grant you one thing and one thing alone.

(Pause) Take a few deep belly breaths.

For this moment let your thoughts float freely.

What would it be?

Just for now, open your mind to the endless possibilities that
could be incorporated into this singular ask.

Would you ask for some thing? Some person? Health? Wealth?
Power? An Experience?
Or would you ask for qualities of heart and mind? Intelligence?
Skill? Courage? Patience? Honor? Freedom? Well-being?
Love?

Psalm 27 is recited from the beginning of the last month before
the New Year, the month of Elul, all the way until Hoshana Rabbah in the midst of Succot. It is a time of asking and seeking. It is
a time to get clear.

What do I really want? What do I really seek?

The High Holy Days (and everything that leads into them) are non-historical and personal Jewish time. They are all about us as individuals. It is not so much about the Jewish people and their movement in history. It is not like Passover in that way. It is all about us. It is all up to us. What are we asking for?

The psalmist answered like this:

Shivti b'veit Adonai kol Yimei Chayai
Lachzot b'noam Adonai ul'vakeir b'heichalo.

To live in the house of Adonai all the days of my life,
To gaze upon the beauty of Adonai, and to frequent God's temple.

Do you know where the house of Adonai exists?
Can you describe the beauty of Adonai?
Do you know what it means to frequent God's temple?

What would it mean for me to ask to live in the house of
   Adonai?
Is it a house with a roof, walls, and a door?
Is it a way of being? A way of feeling?
Is it a way to know that I am whole, free, loved, and safe?

What would it mean to gaze on the beauty of Adonai?
Is that everywhere or somewhere special?
Is that an internal beauty or an external beauty?
What kind of eyes can see the beauty of Adonai?

Where is God's temple? Is it a building? A place? A time? Is it a church, synagogue, mosque, or zendo? Is it a mountain peak or jungle or a rushing river? Is it an orphanage or hospital? Is this God's temple?

What does it mean to live in the house of Adonai?

Is it a sense of being fully alive and never separate?

Is it something like being found and returned home and never feeling lost again?

What are your questions?

What are you asking for?

THE GREAT TURNING

Our practice prepares us to be with the darkness with a soft heart, so that clear vision arises and grows strong. Our practice helps us release attachment to the constricted and fear-based idea that "this is how we always have done it." Knowing the urgency, we remain deeply grateful to be alive in this time when we can take part in the Great Turning (a term coined by David Korten and used by visionary teacher Joanna Macy). We practice to see our choices. We practice to act in alignment with generosity, love, and intentionality. We practice to learn how to serve in joy. As we learn from the sacred Psalms:

We practice to be a like a tree deeply rooted alongside brooks of water, that yields its fruit in due season, and whose leaf never withers . . . (Psalm 1). We practice because we know that the greater reality, the divine breath, the Creator, does not desire wickedness. In fact wickedness is truly of no substance and does not have a permanent place in this reality (Psalm 5:5).

We practice because we can trust kindness. Kindness gives us our voice (Psalm 13).

We practice because the only way to know wholeness and connection is through truthfulness and releasing the desire to possess what is not rightly mine (Psalm 15).

We practice because, despite our inadequacies and limitations, we have been given the power over the rest of creation. Our decisions really matter. Truly, we are only slightly less than the angels and we are crowned with consciousness and the potential for transformation (Psalm 8).

PSALM 30

A poem, a song—
We dedicate this heart, mind, and body—our home on earth—
    to goodness,
Opening and flowing follows constriction, discontent, and gloom.
It is a high and glorious thing to let go of suffering.
Let's all sing to that!!

Exile is short, but love is eternal.
Truly joy can follow weeping as quickly as a new day breaks.
Even though to me, my trouble seems endless.
I think, "I will always be miserable."
But a mountain of confidence and strength resides right here as
    close as my own face.
So I implore the universe:
"Have I not been created to know this—to know and to praise?
    Is this not the destiny of consciousness? To journey back to
    unity?"

I listen for the vibration. It comes as dancing.
My grief is released.
I am wrapped in joy.
In order to witness to this, to honor and praise.
May I never more be silent!

PSALM FOR THE SABBATH DAY—PSALM 92

A student of the way things are unfolding,
grows flexible like a palm tree,
flourishes like a cedar and is as amazing as a redwood.

Planted in the divine soil, ever nourished by roots tapping
    supreme goodness
even in old age she will thrive and see things fresh and new.

She will keep declaring the possibility of liberation from
    suffering.

She is rock-solid in this ever-flowing universe.

PSALM ONE

You shall be like a tree planted by the rivers of water.

A tree—living, breathing, growing, changing with the seasons,
   rooted deep in the earth, crown lifted to the heavens above.
Planted—drawing on the life force, connected, nurtured, stable,
   firm yet able to flex and bend.
Rivers of water—Life flows, sometimes quickly, sometimes slowly,
   sometimes clear and sometimes cloudy, carrying waste one
   day, beloved cargo the next—all going to the great sea.

That brings forth fruit in its season.

The fruit—sweet, ripe, firm, juicy, delicious, colorful, delighting
   the senses.
The fruit—the product, the culmination, the integration, the
   result of so much intelligent determination.

When is the *season* right? Who knows?
Faith. Patience. Honesty. Willingness. Friendship.
These all know.

Whose leaf does not wither.
Is there a tree whose leaf does not wither?
Yes.
The evergreen.
Stately, majestic.
Witness to the changes, sun and snow,
but not shaken.

So generous,
so wide and true.
Spruce, pine, cedar, hemlock,
leaves of resilience,
unending green.
Tiferet.

And whatever one does will succeed

And a true way to measure success.
A deep receptivity to receive it when it arrives,
an expansive definition of it and
compassion for the unfinished,
recognizing the arrival in the departure and the departure in the
    arrival,
as joy enfolds sadness and
happiness cradles each moment of forgetting,
and lifts it back to God.

MIZMOR SHIR LEYOM HASHABBAT: PSALM 92

Joyous Singing on Shabbat
Because we know how good it feels to let go of our constant
    desire for things to be different than they are, and
be at peace with what is here right now.

Joyous singing on Shabbat because we acknowledge, finally,
    that we are not fully in control.
We are not the ones who have the complete plan nor the ones
    who conceive and manage all this giant deep mystery.

Joyous singing on Shabbat
because there is so much to be grateful for.
The world is filled with such delight and beauty,
so much wonder,
such vastness—
And today we can stop long enough to notice.
To remember how big it is and how small we are
and how we are part of it and it is part of us
and how good that feels when we do!

Joyous singing on Shabbat because there is love.
There is faithfulness,
there is gratitude,
there is generosity.
These are the roots of our lives that are planted in the house
    of Endless Spirit.

These are the date palms and the cedars that feed and support us.

We rest on the foundation of rock and rustle in the breeze of
this world.
We sing joyously. It is Shabbat!!

PSALM 18

How do we withstand the trials of being alive?
Where is the resting place amidst the constant change and
    confusion?

To seek to serve,
to try to love,
to hope to feel a greater Love—that is our home, our place of
    refuge, our comfort, and our strength.
We learn from David—king, warrior, lover, sinner, singer of
    songs—a man who had plenty of trials and tribulations.
"God's love is my stronghold," says David.
Sometimes, God's love appears only when we are desperate and
    feel encircled by the bonds of death itself.
And God appears like a blazing light—shaking the earth and
    rocking our mountains.
A huge force, grasping thunderbolts, scattering arrows, and
    scooping us out of the deepest waters . . .
Flying through our lives, mounted on a cherub (what a sight!),
    swooping through our fears on the wings of wind . . .
Releasing us into a spacious consciousness, where we are safe
    and at ease.
Sometimes I experience God's love when I understand things.
I understand the law of cause and effect.
I understand that now we have choices that shape our future
    experience. Things are not random.
My efforts toward goodness and devotion bear blessed fruit

and the result of hatred and ill will is more of the same.

For You, my God,

Will light the candle of my spirit.

You will dispel the darkness of my hopelessness.

You are a shield in my anxiety, a rock in my unsteadiness, a refuge in my confusion, a belt of strength around my weak center.

Your power broadens my stride and my stance so that my steps are confident and relaxed.

All my difficulties,

all my fears, frustrations, temptations,

Turn out to be insubstantial.

Like dust blowing in the wind,

Like mud washing through the streets.

Violence and hurting need not be my path.

I can rise above my petty struggles and complaints.

I yearn to let everyone know and understand how I have found peace.

I want everyone to hear how the obstacles to happiness have been overturned before me.

I want to sing and shout.

Because I entrusted my life to You, to your loving kindness and care.

GUIDED EVENING PRAYER

This might be something to do with a partner. One reads the script and the other enacts the instruction and then you can switch. If you are alone you might want to record this in your sweetest voice and then play for yourself.

Borchu—
is a gathering in call and response, signifying relationship and
    exchange
between each other,
between the finite and the Infinite,
the known and the Mystery,
the separate and the unified,
between energy, matter, and awareness.

Let us unify body and mind with the breath.
Let us experiment with very simple movements guided by the
    breath.

I Invite you to stand and
feel the earth under your feet.
Move your feet and feel your feet in relation to the earth.
Find stillness and softness in standing. Knees can be soft.
Relaxed standing with minimum effort.
It has been a very long day with lots of sitting.
Let your weight be distributed evenly—front and back, side
    to side.
Let your head gently lift and open upwards.
Become aware of your front, your back, your sides.

Natural breathing, eyes open and soft.

Whole body breathing: allow the energy to move evenly in and out
of your body.
Bend knees slightly on the exhale and straighten on the inhale.

Central channel breathing: hands move slowly up the center line
of the body and out the crown of the head, fountaining out,
separating and gently flowing back to earth; then circulating
back with the next inhalation.
Notice relationship, exchange, mutuality . . . earth and heaven
uniting

Three centers: energy/power center in belly; heart center; wisdom
center.
Each is a center of connection to Divine life force, to each other
and ourselves.
Rock back and forth.
Start by centering in the earth and opening to the heavens,
Breathing in and out through the nose.

Hands at power center: palms down to start and spiral upwards as
center opens and then closes as the hands return to starting posi-
tion; when you are ready move to heart center and finally to the
head center.

Bowing: surrender (join the winning side)—release ego, agenda,
getting it right, judgement, competition, control—yikes!
Let gravity do the work.
Honor your range of motion. Let knees bend as needed.
Neck and head release first, slowly, breathing, vertebrae by verte-
brae. Down, down.
Linger, soften and return—restack the spine.

Borchu
A great pool of blessing

Braicha
Bracha

Wisdom brings the night
and propels this earth around this sun,
ordaining that day follows night and night follows day.
Each is different and each is blessed.
Day and night,
our eternal and forever rhythm, dance, breath.
Through you we plot our days.

Tamid yimloch alyenu l'olam vaed
Baruch ata adonai Hamaariv aravim

AHAVAT OLAM

Can we take in eternal love? Forever love? Everlasting love?
Can we hold love in our hearts for as long as we can hold our
   breath?
One inhale, one exhale.
Can we just feel loved?
Not just good enough, not just okay for now, but deeply loved.

In your imagination recall the face of someone who loves you—a
   teacher, a pet, a grandparent, a child.
Drink it in, a moment of love, a snapshot of a loving glance.
Let it fill you completely as far as your fingertips and the tips of
   your toes.
Eternal Love
For always.
When we go to sleep and when we wake up.
Underneath our actions and thoughts, our theories and practicali-
   ties. In our words, our walks, our whimsies.
Love.
This is our meditation.
Full-blown love.
No limits.
No excuses.
No exceptions

After all these years, the earth never says to the sun, you owe me.
Think how a love like that can light up the world. (Hafiz)

We open to the deepest listening of our beings when we chant
   Shma Yisrael. We address our own souls. We address our clear-
   est minds and wisest selves.
Echad is One. It is where we are rooted. It is where we find ourselves and lose our selves at the same time. It is the great love
   that can light up the world.
We call ourselves out of our petty preferences to the endlessly
   wide and wild place of One.

A LIST I MADE INSPIRED BY A POEM BY WALT WHITMAN

This is what you shall do...
Learn how to breathe deeply.
Forgive everyone.
Don't ever worry about how things are going to turn out.
Don't criticize yourself, your partner, your children, or anyone else.
Stretch your body from the place of stability.
Forget about being a "good" anything.
Forget about being an anything.
Always find things to laugh about as long as they don't hurt
    anyone.
Especially laugh at yourself.
Drink really good tea and eat really good chocolate.
Don't do things that make you sick or mad or stupid.
Get a pedicure every month.
Use less of whatever it is.
Play with the children; really play with the children. Let the
    children teach you how to play.
Sing and dance.
Trust your intuition, your gut, your heart.
Soften.
Soften.
Soften.
Remember how blessed you are.
Be grateful for the senses that work, for food, clothing, shelter.

Advocate for a clean, just, and peaceful neighborhood, community, country, world.

Stop feeling so guilty.

Remember it is not always your fault.

Pay attention to the seasons, the sunlight, the moon, the bird.

Pay attention to the miracle of standing, walking, lying down.

Feel it.

Smile more.

Remember you are old enough to stop doing things that you don't want to do.

Remember you don't have to do things or be with people that deplete you.

It is okay to daydream as long as you know you are daydreaming.

Remember that everyone is just who they are.

Don't take it personally.

DOWN DOG

Place your fingers carefully.
Hug the muscles to the bone.
Heads of the arm bones back, back, back.
Stretch from the heart.
Heart open.
Heart closed.
More heart.
Soften the heart.
The back of the heart.
Yes.
Offer the heart.

This is the way I love to pray.

UHRDVA DANURASANA—THE WHEEL

Lie on your back.
Place your feet on the floor—knees pointing straight up to the
   ceiling.
The black rubber mat is covering the smooth pine slats.
Bring your hands next to your shoulders—fingers pointing away
   from your face.

Expand your inner body.
Breathe into the universe as it shows up here, in your innards.
Inner body.
My abode.
Holy breath, sacred light.
Breathe.
Holy light pours in from the mind of God filling organs, sinews,
   cells.

Make more space for Me!!

Make more space.

I want to dwell within you, I want to dwell among you.

Press the heads of your arm bones down down down
With determination.
No harshness.
No rush.
Pure pressure.

Press into your hands and feet and rise to the top of your head.

Lift your chin away from your chest.
Open your throat.
No words.
No words.
Not a syllable.
Only a breath
Halleluiah.

Hollow your armpits and plug the shoulders into the back.
Make more space for ME!!

Now lift your heart.
Extend your heart toward your face.
Toward the face of God.
Toward me.
Breathe.

Heart lifts.
Extends.
Breathes.
Grazes heaven.
Halleluiah. Halleluiah!!!

YOU ARE STANDING

Atem Nitzavim Hayom
Kulchem Lifnei Adonai Eloheichem
—Deuteronomy 29:9

Nitzavim Standing
in the Presence,
Assembled
Atem You, you, you.
Hayom Today. Now. This moment. This in breath. This sensation.
    This sound. This word. This image. This thought.
Now.
Kulchem All of you.
Every one,
dead alive,
high low,
known unknown,
inside outside,
back front,
hidden revealed,
near far,
remembered forgotten.
All Everything.
All together.
Lifnei Before—In the face of—In-side
Yud Hay Vav Hay
Being becoming being
Eloheichem

Your God
Your deepest possibility your commitment
Your hope
Your promise
Your reality
Everything Nothing All change
All vibration, all Love, all Power, all benevolence, all limits
NOW.

SOLSTICE IN NEW ENGLAND

It was so dark this morning—solstice at the new moon. It's darker in New England when there is no snow. I don't remember when it was this late in the year and there hadn't been any snow. As I passed the UMass stadium, there were a bunch of cars parked and then I saw people standing around in the dark morning. They were standing at the sun wheel that Judy Young had built. It was a ritual gathering for the winter solstice.

As I rode along I passed the home of Rabbi Edelman, the rabbi of the Lubavitch community. He had a six-foot-high electric menorah on his lawn. Six lights were lit. The menorah was a marker on the road as we passed by in accord with the mandate to publicize the miracle of Hanukkah. The menorah serves as a witness of one community to the whole world that miracles do happen.

I turned, as I always do after the Coolidge Bridge, on to Bridge Street, heading for the synagogue and morning meditation. This morning I noticed the two Christmas tree and wreath merchants. Spruce trees waiting to be part of the magic of Christmas when homes are transformed into fantasy lands of magic and warmth—or so we hope.

It is the dark of the moon and the sun. We are tenderly aware of relationships and cycles. Human beings inhabiting the spheres—earth circling sun, moon circling earth. What does it mean? Who knows? All we see is waning and waxing light over a day, a month, a year. This is the universal truth. We are all part of this flow. No matter who or where we are. And we gather to proclaim our awareness of the passage of time. We gather to huddle together in our amazement, gratitude, awe, and vulnerability. In any moment that I know how vulnerable I am, how fragile life is, in that moment I am free. I am no longer a stranger and neither are you. We are miracles. It could have been otherwise. This is not of our making but we can bring our attention to it. We can mark a spot in these cycles and say: "We see. We know. And we decide to rededicate ourselves in this moment to what is good. We turn ourselves toward the light. This is our gift as humans and our choice."

Everywhere humans are, we take the universal and make it particular. But we often forget that it is universal. We like to own things so much that we think we can own God, too. This is the great religious problem.

So, here I am about to teach to a group of Jews in a synagogue who have gathered to meditate. And I feel compelled to remind them and myself that we are gathering to pay attention to another universal cycle, like that of the moon and the earth in their pulsation and rotation. This is the cycle of the breath—in and out, a perfect circle.

And the breath is not Jewish or Buddhist or American or Chinese or white or black any more than the new moon or the solstice. Noticing the breath and returning to the sense of being breathed with an intention of renewal, remembering, connecting to this very moment and to our own goodness, the clarity of awareness itself, the non-judging, non-harming quality of presence in this moment.

We acknowledge the paradox of particular and universal. We love our particular story, language, forms. Through them we touch the whole. And we love that there are so many forms reaching toward the One. It is the way it is here on earth. In the words of Desmond Tutu: "My humanity is bound up in yours, for we can only be human together."

A MOMENT OF MINDFULNESS IS A MOMENT OF COMPASSION—EITHER WAY, A BLESSING

Coming home to this moment.
Recognizing we are alive. And that is good.
Let's take a moment to receive what is here.
I invite everyone to take a conscious breath and just feel. Whatever feeling feels like to you.
Breathing in. Breathing out.
Feeling sensations. Warmth. Coolness. Tingling, Pulsing, Vibration . . . Hearing sounds as they arise and pass.
Seeing colors and shapes.
Our benevolent awareness is blessing each moment.
Receiving each moment just as it is.
Like a clear mirror.
We rest in the light that is within us, within each other.
In this moment feeling beautiful.
Just for a moment
setting critique, judgment, comparing aside.
Practicing blessing just what is right now.

In a world; in a mind—of frantic striving to know, make and have,
Just to be, to attend, to wait, to receive in stillness
is healing; is loving; is freeing; is sacred.
In our world; in our mind
stillness is radical.
Stillness is wild.

Breathing in, breathing out. Saying to ourselves: I am alive. Alive.
In good company.
Safe.
Happy. Peaceful. At ease.
Blessing what is right now.
I relax.
Breathing in. I am alive
Breathing out. I am blessed
I soften.
I receive.
This moment as it is.
We are blessing and being blessed.

BLESSING PRACTICE

Miles Krassen defines Hasidut as the science of love. Therefore to be a Hasid is to be someone working to deepen his or her capacity to love. The question that frequently arises when we read mystical sources about union and unity is: "Why was separation from the One really necessary?" My favorite response to that question is: "There was no room for love without separation." There was no room for the *middot,* the divine qualities, without the separation because they all involve some coin of relationship, some kind of return, and some form of connection. That is the nature of generosity, love, and kindness.

The great paradox is that we are always returning to what is already here. So what is here? The infinite qualities of lovingkindness, joy, compassion, and peacefulness. How do I remember that? How do I remember in the midst of my life? That is the fundamental question. Practices of many kinds are attempts to answer the question "How do I remember?"

I invite us to practice invoking blessing. Rabbi Jeff Roth developed this practice over his many years of teaching. Blessing helps us connect with our deepest desires and intentions. Blessing is a way to open the heart and plant seeds of love and kindness, joy and peace within. First we set an intention. We gather energy and energy disperses. Again and again, we meet dispersion, coming back and remembering the intention, the *kavanna.* We do this in order to settle down, to settle the mind. We can use the breath and the step. We can also use phrases. The blessing practice is in effect sparse, pared down, repetitive prayer that is said internally.

We plant an intention by saying a phrase. At the same time we cultivate a felt sense of the quality, allowing that felt sense to wash over us—if we can. We cannot assure that anything is going to happen. We cannot assure what is going to come. We may open to prayer and find a shadow. We may see the opposite of what we invoke. We may see a contraction. We may see a fear. We may see running away. We see what arises. We bring the same quality of kindness to whatever arises. When what is arising is seen plainly, it is just what it is. It is acceptable.

I find it is most valuable to first bring the qualities of loving kindness to myself. For some people that does not work well, and they prefer to begin by imagining someone in their life who opens their heart. The blessing practice is an offering. It is relationship practice. One offers a blessing to another. It begins in separation but leads to connection. When the heart is filled with kindness or compassion, joy or peace, the divine qualities, boundaries and directions do disappear. These divine qualities are no respecter of borders. They know no stranger. Blessings overflow the artificial banks of identity.

It is important to feel relaxed and comfortable in your seat. Relax your face, relax your heart. Soften your belly. Allow yourself to sit without tension but with a certain amount of alertness. Feel your breath in your body, and then specifically in your heart. Have a sense of breathing in and out of your own heart. You may feel your heart beating. Acknowledge the breath of life. See how your heart rises and falls. Now, imagine the face of a loved one or someone who lights up your life, someone who has given you a gift of kindness. Or imagine their presence or hearing their voice. Just allow yourself to feel that kindness. Let it saturate your being. Feel the sense of ease, acceptance, and total love in your body. You can offer your blessings toward that person or you can offer those blessings towards yourself, just opening your own heart to your own presence.

Offer these words silently, "May I be blessed with *Chesed*—kindness, love. May I be blessed with *Rachamim*—compassion. May I be blessed with *Simchah*—joy. May I be blessed with *Shalom*—peace, wholeness, equanimity."

We are not trying to force anything. Rather we are evoking the felt sense of *chesed*—kindness or the felt sense of *rachamim*, compassion, being quiet, present, still, in the face of pain, in the face of suffering. Being with each word as it is said. May I be blessed with *chesed, rachamim, simchah, shalom*. May you be blessed with *chesed, rachamim, simchah, shalom*.

You may want to offer this to a child or grandchild if that is the face that opens your heart. Choose someone that is easy to bless. When you offer a blessing to yourself, remember that there is no one on this earth who deserves a blessing more than you do. Whatever flows into one being will flow to all those that surround that being. When you offer a blessing to anyone, you are being blessed. *Simcha*, joy, is not frantic or manic, but an expansion, an enjoying the joy of allowing one's merits, one's successes, one's existence to be celebrated in an expanded way. May I be blessed with *simchah* and may you just feel *simchah* in your body. May you be blessed with *shalom*—peace, well-being, equanimity, equilibrium, capacity, the spaciousness of mind and heart to hold difference, to hold conflict, to dance with paradox, to meet life without fear or hatred. May I be blessed with *shalom*, a deep, deep, abiding peace in myself, a feeling of *shalom* in the cells of the body. *Shalom* throughout the neural pathways of my life, of the life of the species. May you be blessed with *shalom*.

Each time you invoke a word, connect to the felt sense of that word. Each time you offer it to anyone, feel your own body, your own breath, your own face, your own light. Bring your awareness to yourself or to the person that you are envisioning, the person you are holding in your heart. May you be blessed with *chesed*. May you be blessed with *rachamim*. May you be blessed with *simchah*. May you be blessed with *shalom*. If it is too much to say "may you be blessed," you can just use the words by themselves.

You might want to just try to do each phrase on a breath, maybe two breaths. Try not to linger too long, just keep moving and cycling through the phrases. You might find that you forget the words or the order. You might find that you drift off. You might just fall into the rabbit hole of complete forgetfulness or distraction. When you wake up, there is a moment of awareness; a moment of return. With kindness and gentleness, come back to *chesed, rachamim, simchah, and shalom*. We are planting seeds deep in the earth. We are practicing *t'shuva* again and again and again and again.

PRIESTLY BLESSING MEDITATION

(This is an alternative to the blessing practice "May you be blessed with chesed . . .")

Yivarecheha Adonai Veyishmerecha
Yaer Adonai Panav Elecha Vechunecha
Yisa Adonai Panav Elecha v'Yasem lecha Shalom

According to the priestly blessing, what are the qualities of blessing that we seek to plant in our lives?

May I feel *safe.*
May I feel *kindness.*
May I feel *peaceful.*

Can we take these qualities into our hearts like seeds planted in the ground of our lives?

Can we allow each phrase to float on a breath that seeps deeply into our consciousness?

When we say a phrase we imagine the sense of *safety and protection* rooting in our bodies. *(yivarechecha adonai v'yishmerecha)*

We imagine *kindness* swelling our hearts and making them luminous. *(yaer adonai panav elecha vechunecha)*

We imagine tension, stress, and conflict in our muscles and nerves dissolving and leaving us whole and at *peace. (yisa adonai panav elecha v'yasem lecha shalom)*

We continue reciting the phrases as a direction to embody these wholesome and divine qualities.

We now turn the object of our blessing to our loved ones. As we visualize those we wish to include in the blessing, we continue to direct our attention to our inner felt sense of these qualities. You may wish to imagine holding your open palms above your own head and above the head of someone you are blessing in the traditional gesture of blessing.

May I feel *safe*.
May I feel *kindness*.
May I feel *peaceful*.

MEDITATION ON THE HAND BEFORE RITUAL WASHING INSPIRED BY JOANNA MACY

This is a great practice prior to a meal, either at the Seder—which does include two ritual hand washings—or Friday night dinner, or any other time we can take to contemplate our own and each other's hands.

Take a few deep breaths and gaze upon your hands.

Notice the shape, the color, the lines, spots, and veins. Notice the luminous quality of the nails. Notice soft spots, the tender spots.

Now take your left hand and explore your right hand. Feel the bones, the skin, rough or smooth. Feel the ridges, the hollow spaces. Feel the warmth of this hand. Notice any variations in texture, temperature.

Move the fingers. Stretch and open this hand. Make a fist. Feel the power in this hand.

Contemplate the miracle of this hand.

Think of the journey this hand has taken from infant, to child and to adult. From youth to age. From innocence to competence. From vulnerability to vulnerability. How much this hand had to learn—to hold, to feed, to draw, write, zip and button, to use a myriad of tools, to type, to cook, to fix, to caress, to soothe, to play music and create beauty.

Now turn to your neighbor and hold each other's hand. See how similar it is to yours and see how different.

See if you can prepare your hands for a blessing of water, of purification, of lifting up in awareness and attention, in gratitude and wonder, in respect and love.

We will now pass the bowl and wash each other's hands. All the while wishing each other well. Wishing each other safety and well being, wishing each other strength and dexterity, protection and kindness.

May these hands receive God's blessings and bounty.
May these hands be generous and kind to both friend and
stranger.
May these hands open in generosity to those in need.
May these hands receive the support of friends and strangers.
May these hands trust and inspire.
May they create and delight.
May they merit to perform deeds of goodness, compassion,
healing, and love.

BORAY NEFASHOT RABOT—SHORT GRACE AFTER EATING A MEAL WITHOUT BREAD

Thank you
Creator of the many beings who live on this earth
All of them—whole,
All of them—partial.
For the gift of this creation
We acknowledge You—
Maker of time, space, and energy.

THE TORAH AND THE JEWS

The deer at the river yearning.
The Jews at the sea singing.
Thank you for holy books,
stories of water and wilderness, love and hate, jealousy and
    courage.
Thank you for the letters and spaces—pathways where we meet
    ourselves and find you through each other.

Thank you for the Torah.
We don't have to invent our own memories.
We are given bundles of mistakes and suitcases of forgiveness.

Thank you for the Torah.
We can always be leaving Haran or Egypt or gathering at Sinai
    or wandering in the desert or entering the land.

Thank you for the Torah where we are always singing, weeping,
    dancing, praying—making war and peace, having children,
    dying, looking for a way home.

Thank you for the Torah.
Endless keys opening endless doors of hearts and minds, teach-
    ing us, loving us, because we are human—
frail and powerful,
wise and weak,
faithful and forgetting.

Thank you for the Torah.

WHEN I THINK I AM RIGHT

Here is a story about telling a story that I used to introduce mindfulness meditation to a group of rabbis shortly after the first Obama election. I was telling a story I had told a few times before, and I understood it as a good description of the nature of the mind, specifically about how the mind tells itself stories in order to understand reality that actually may have little relation to the truth. Sometimes, especially after being in silence without outside stimulation for a while, we come to realize that the mind has a mind of its own. "I," whoever that is, is certainly not controlling "my" thoughts.

The story was about an experience I had on an extended silent retreat shortly after 9/11. I was walking past the home of the lead meditation teacher who lived next door to the retreat center. I noticed an American flag waving on his property. I thought to myself, "How strange. I can't imagine this highly esteemed spiritual teacher is going to succumb to the knee-jerk patriotic display of the flag in the post 9/11 universe." I started trying to explain to myself what this might mean, including the desire to fit in with the rural population that surrounded the retreat center, to purchase some credibility in the eyes of the neighbors and so on. I had it fairly well rationalized when, on the way back from my walk, I noticed that the flag was not at my teacher's home at all but at someone else's.

That story was one illustration among many, and at the end of the talk to the rabbis, a young woman rabbi from the Midwest approached me looking extremely upset and angry. She said that

172

she did not appreciate the trashing of the flag implied in my story. She added that she was an American and had voted for John McCain, which she considered to be a perfectly responsible choice as a Jew, a rabbi, an American. My story made her feel like she did not belong in this particular community if she were not an Obama voter. I was taken aback. My own assumptions and politics had clearly sifted through what I thought was a "spiritual" teaching experience. I knew enough in that moment to say that I was really sorry to have upset her, and that I would like to give the matter some more thought. I later apologized for my bias and for my lack of awareness. I truly wanted her to feel comfortable in this group. I challenged myself to truly respect someone whose politics were that different from mine. *Pirkei Avot 4:1* asks us: "Who is wise?" Then it answers: "The one who learns from everyone."

It was not pleasant to have a mirror brought up to my face, which revealed my own blind spots. I still think it is a good story, but I am continually challenged to tell it in a way that does not humiliate or belittle those whose views differ from my own. A teacher has to open wide embracing arms to every student that shows up and sincerely wants to learn. This particular student did want to learn. She stayed around and did learn. I learned from her, I suspect, even more than she from me.

LAMDEINI—TEACH ME!

Teach me, O God, a blessing, a prayer
On the mystery of a withered leaf so fair,
On the freedom to see, to sense,
To breathe, to know, to hope, to despair.

Teach my lips a blessing, a hymn of praise,
As each morning and night
You renew Your days,
Lest my day be today as the one before;
Lest routine set my ways.

I think that the above poem, written by Israeli poet Leah Goldberg, is a magnificent introduction to mindfulness in a Jewish context. I heard it sung by Cantor Benjie Schiller at a retreat of the first cantors' cohort of the Institute for Jewish Spirituality. I have been on the faculty of the Institute teaching mindfulness meditation and yoga. The first time I heard these words tears came to my eyes. Why did it touch me so? Let's look at the words:
Lamdeini Elohai. Teach me, O God. A person is speaking to God and asking to learn something. *Lamed–mem–dalet* are letters that form a very common Hebrew root seen in many words. A pupil is a *talmid*, from this same root. Torah study is *Talmud Torah*. It can also refer to learning science or general studies. The speaker in this text addresses God but does not ask for information, concepts, arguments, or reasons. "Teach me a blessing, a prayer on the mystery of a withered leaf on ripened fruit so fair." What kind of learning is that?

I would suggest that our poet is seeking to be taught heart learning. This is the kind of learning that takes time and patience and a particular orientation. It is not often taught in schools. It is not usually prized in the mainstream media. Often I am too busy to pay attention to a withered leaf or a piece of ripe fruit. I tend to ignore the leaf (how many withered leaves are lying around at any given moment?); I might consume the fruit if I am hungry and it looks good. I will judge the fruit or the leaf based on its utility to me. If it is useful, it will become part of my experience, if not, I do not need to embrace it in my glance.

The first few lines of the poem suggest we can be taught to have the patience, the interest, and the wonder to pause and ponder the mystery of a withered leaf or the *nogah*—the radiance—of a piece of ripe fruit. When I ask to learn a mystery, I am asking for a revelation of that which is hidden. I bring myself into a relationship with a leaf or a piece of fruit—or it might be a face, a word, a lump of clay, a note of music, an in breath, a feeling of love or sadness flowing through my veins, a very old wound that is now fresh in my flesh. I bring myself into relationship, and I wait. I release any certainty that I know what this is about. I am intimate with this moment. The willingness to drop *knowing* what this is allows what this is to *be known*. The knowing is not abstract or conceptual. It is sensual. It is immediate and connected. As long as I know this old leaf has no value or this piece of fruit will taste like this, or this is just another breath, big deal, I have closed off the possibility of really learning anything. All of science and art are based on a willingness to be open to mystery. What is creativity? What is discovery? Is it not the "freedom to see, to sense, to breathe, to know, to hope, to despair"?

The same is true in the field of the human heart. As long as I am convinced that I am an angry person or a fearful person, or my neighbor will never like me, or I can never forgive someone who hurt me, there is no mystery. It is all set, known, determined.

As long as I am caught in absolutes and certainties, perfect, solid conclusions, there is no freedom. One day follows another and is exactly the same. (*Yomi hayom kitmol shilshom*—my day today *is* as the one before.)

Is there another way to be? The poet suggests that there is. She is asking for the ability to be fully present to what is true in this moment—"to see, to sense, to breathe." When we develop this capacity to truly be present to our experience, we see that everything passes, that there is nothing completely fixed or separate. I rest in the awareness of feelings that arise and pass. I see mistakes occur, grief and despair come and go as do joy and peace. All things are part of my experience, but they do not define who I am. Therein lies the possibility for renewal, change, surprise. *Who I am* becomes the greatest unfolding mystery. As Albert Einstein said: "I have no special talent. I am just passionately curious."

The word *lamdeini* echoes another term, *hitlamdut,* which is known in the world of *Musar,* Jewish ethical development, as a core concept. It is the willingness to investigate and open to what is truly happening within our experience. *Hitlamdut*—curiosity, investigation—the willingness to see something fresh is the axis upon which our character is refined.

What *is* the mystery of a withered leaf? A ripened fruit? The mystery is revealed when I am present. The poet is asking to learn how to show up. How to be really present. This is a serious practice in a world crammed with accelerating addictive distractions. When I behold the withered leaf, it is a contemplation of its ending. The tendency of the mind is to run from the ends of things and to embrace the beginnings. The withered leaf is not separate from the new leaf. They are parts of each other. Similarly the poet asks for the freedom to hope *and* despair. *L'hekashel* translated as despair can also mean to fail. Can we learn to be with our failures as well as with our hopes and see that they do not define us? It all depends on our attitude. The attitude of presence is soft and non-judgmental. It is accepting and compassionate, patient and kind. It is forgiveness itself. And who does not continually need forgiveness?

In Deuteronomy, we read one of the most memorable lines in the Torah: "I have put before you life and death, blessing and curse. Choose life . . ." This is what Leah Goldberg is praying for—the capacity to choose life. She sees that death is all around in the routine, avoidance, fear of the unpleasant, the reactivity based on old stories and traumas that shadow our lives. Choose life means step into the mystery. Step into the unknown. Stop and ask about the withered leaf. Pause and look into the splendor of the ripe fruit and see it is only here for a moment of glory. It, too, is part of the stream of day and night, year ending, year beginning. Stay present. Wake up. Choose life. Life is fluid. It is free. It is greater than our concepts or constraints.

This attitude of newness and forgiveness carries us into the next moment. Mystery is spacious enough to embrace the innocent child and the very old person along with everything in between. It remembers that the ripeness contains the withered and the withered contains the ripeness. Mystery is great enough to be intimate with hope and despair, in breath and out breath, success and failure, gain and loss, illness and health, joy and sorrow. Mystery is great enough to contain it all.

Teach my lips a blessing, a hymn of praise—*bracha v'shir halel.* This is the attitude we choose toward our life. This is the attitude that has learned that only humility can reveal possibility. We enter into this moment with a heart that yearns to be free, lips willing to sing and praise, and minds open to learning from the divine teacher.

—*lamdeini elohay!*

MY RABBINATE AT 71

It seems a good time to reflect on my life and my rabbinate.
While it is thirty-one years since I graduated the Reconstructionist Rabbinical College, I have spent my whole life working with
and for the Jewish community. I was a Hebrew schoolteacher and
a day school teacher, a community relations organizer, an editor, a
Hillel director and supervisor, a graduate student in Jewish studies,
and a congregational rabbi. Now I am a consultant and a spiritual
director. Mostly I teach mindfulness meditation (and a little yoga)
to Jewish professionals and laypeople, and I do a lot of sitting with
people and helping them chart their spiritual journeys.

I went to high school and college in pre-feminist days. While
Judaism and things of a spiritual nature were my passion from
childhood, there was no category for even thinking about equality
of the sexes or the possibility of a female rabbi. In fact, in my family there was really only one conceivable, respectable, and practical
profession for a woman—becoming a teacher. So, it is with irony
(or destiny) that I really have been a teacher my whole life. It is
the ribbon that ties all the different roles and tasks together.

What has changed over time is what I teach and why I teach.
My teaching today has very little to do with content. I am inter-
ested in helping people wake up in their lives. My fundamental
goal is to encourage people to see that they have more choices
than they think, and that they need not be victims of every
thought or feeling they have. I teach awakened attention, in the
moment, to one's experience, without judgment. It is a practice

and a process that has the power to free us from our unconscious habits and sense of disconnection.

I am very vulnerable when I teach. I talk about intention, choice, kindness, and happiness. These things are so basic they may seem simplistic. However, they are infinitely complex in their simplicity. I work to structure settings where people feel safe enough to allow themselves to focus on things that are close to the bone, things that really matter in their lives, patterns of thought and behavior that cause a lot of suffering. I encourage people to sit with what arises. To just sit—not to rush in and judge, condemn, get rid of or fix. I invite people to pay attention to the power of stillness to hold the difficult, and to become aware of the transformation that occurs when we open in friendliness toward our own experience rather than conduct an inner war on our minds and hearts.

How do I prepare for this work? Mostly by being with the content of my own mind and seeing my own weaknesses, habits, and stuck places. I prepare to teach kindness by cultivating kindness in my own life and seeing how fretfully difficult it is. This kind of teaching is compelling to me.

How do I dare to teach what I have so clearly not perfected? How can I teach gratitude when I know that it is only in rare moments that I remember to be grateful? How can I teach generosity when I know how withholding I am? How can I teach patience when I know so well what it feels like to be irritable and internally demanding?

This is the honest part of the practice and the teaching. It is a path, a mysterious process to become an awake being, a Jew discovering the *tzelem elohim* and facing the *tzel,* the shadow that obstructs the shining forth of the pure soul. The miracle of the work is that I am never alone. I am part of something vastly greater than myself. It is very precious. I am indeed grateful.

QUESTIONS: SEEKING THE SEEKER

Here are some questions to open your mind:
Who are you?
Who is breathing now?
Who is thinking now?
Who is sensing and listening now?
To whom is whatever is happening now happening?
Is this you?
Is this who you are?
Who do you take yourself to be?
How often is I, me, or mine in your thinking/in your speaking?
Do you have peace of mind when you think I, me, or mine?
What does it feel like to drop I, me, or mine?

I was the rabbi of two different congregations over the course
of seventeen years. Being a rabbi gave me a great sense of being
someone. In fact, that was a big reason for becoming a rabbi. I
believed that if I became a rabbi it would indicate that I was a
good and worthy human being. I am still a rabbi in the sense that
no one took away my diploma, and I still do what rabbis do—
teach Judaism. But I am not the rabbi to those people in that
place, and I do not work for a congregation. The language here
is instructive. A lot of rabbis say they have a congregation. They
often call it *their* congregation. Sometimes they refer to *their*
board or *their* treasurer. There is a sense of comfort and security
in possession. However, is it true? Do we own our positions,
our communities, and our roles? Many rabbis that I have known

have had *their* congregations ask them to find another job.

I am walking down the street and meet someone. She asks me: "Have you retired?" "No," I say. Then she asks, "Are you on sabbatical" "No, I'm not." "Well, what are you doing, Rabbi?" "I am working for a national organization that helps Jewish leaders develop their spiritual lives—rabbis, cantors, educators, lay leaders." "Hmmm, that's interesting."

These interactions may sprout thoughts in the mind that bring suffering and judgment. Isn't the rabbi that does bar mitzvahs every week and is called late at night to go to the hospital a real rabbi? Am I a phony? Well, if I am not "the rabbi" in this definition then who am I? Do I have the courage to open into the space of not knowing, of not having a fixed and solid identity? When I do, it is like free fall. It feels good. It doesn't matter who I am because there is no absolute permanent solid ME. There are actions and words and thoughts and a great space that holds it all. There are conditions and causes that are impacting on each other. There are my intentions to be of service in the world and to my people. There is awareness of what is occurring and how it is connected to what has just occurred and what will come next. This describes my experience. Yet, I share the habit of imagining a self that is usually striving to be better than it is, a self that is not quite measuring up to some imagined standard. Usually this makes me feel bad.

Seeing the "I" pop up is the first step. The second is remembering that this way of looking at things usually brings a trail of anxiety and conflict in its wake. Third is remembering that these thoughts are not true or real.

Jumping on the "I, me, or mine" train, tends to initiate a giant detour away from the desired destination. What if the thought arises that someone doesn't like me? Or that I am not good enough at this or that? Or that I spent too much money? These thoughts can engender a lot of blaming of myself or others.

However, when there is awareness of this constructed self, without judgment or shame, the pain releases. The heart releases, the trapdoor opens, something erases a line in the box we have drawn around who we are. We step out into possibility, infinity, potential, wonder. A desire for the wholesome intentions, responsibility, connection, and commitment remain. But these are grounded in the dynamic of relationship. They are not boxes.

A lot of spiritual practice is aimed at helping the heart release by reducing the identification with the small and ever active I, me, and mine. Sometimes it is a yielding to a greatness that simply overwhelms the little self. Sometimes it is seeing through the solidity of the self again and again.

There is always the danger in spiritual systems, however, that a new identity will be erected. A new I, me, or mine that must be defended at all costs. This temptation answers a deep desire for the known and the secure. It is in an abiding contest with the unknowable, the mystery. The history of religion reenacts this story in every generation.

The Jewish mystics see a relationship between two Hebrew words that have the same letters. The order of the letters makes the difference. It is how you hold your experience. *Aleph Nun Yud* spells *Ani*, which means I. *Aleph Yud Nun* spells *Ayin*, which is the ultimate name of ultimate reality. *Ani* releases into *Ayin*. In any moment. The known releases into the unknown, the controlled into the uncontrolled. It takes a lot of courage not to know.

It takes a lot of courage to be willing to ask the right questions.

MAKE ME A NURSING TREE

Make me a nursing tree.
When I get old and die, let my bark decay in the wet earth and
   let huckleberries, bright green heart-shaped leaves and irides-
   cent moss grow to cover me.
Then, let new saplings sprout in the thick dank soil, full of hope-
   ful, tender shoots.
Let me be fertile in ideas, in offspring, remembered for my kindness and generosity,
Remembered for humor and courage and for not complaining
   too much and for not hating anyone.

ALSO BY SHEILA WEINBERG

Surprisingly Happy: An Atypical Religious Memoir, White River Press, 2010.

Preparing the Heart: Meditations for Jewish Spiritual Practice, (audio) Institute for Jewish Spirituality, jewishspirituality.org, 2005.

CPSIA information can be obtained
at www.ICGtesting.com
Printed in the USA
FFOW04n0719300417
35021FF

9 781887 043311